Preparation for Esthetics Licensure Exam

Second Edition © 2007 Pivot Point International Inc.

ISBN-13: 978-0-9742723-6-8
ISBN-10: 0-9742723-6-1

© 2004 Pivot Point International Inc.
Third printing

This publication may not be reproduced or quoted in whole or in part in printed or electronic form, or used in presentations on radio, television, videotape, film or other electronic means without written permission from Pivot Point International, Inc. All rights reserved.

1560 Sherman Avenue
Evanston, IL 60201
1.800.886.4247
www.pivot-point.com

Contents

A Special Note to Students 4

Chapter 1, Personal Development 8

Chapter 2, Professional Development 14

Chapter 3, Business Basics 18

Chapter 4, Skin Care Center Ecology 24

Chapter 5, Anatomy 33

Chapter 6, Electricity and Electrical Equipment 50

Chapter 7, Chemistry 59

Chapter 8, Skin Physiology 68

Chapter 9, Client Care 77

Chapter 10, Facials 84

Chapter 11, Hair Removal. 92

Chapter 12, Makeup 100

Chapter 13, Advanced Treatments 108

Chapter 14, Estheticians in the Medical Field. 117

Final Exam 126

Answer Key and Page References
for Chapters 1-14. 143

Answer Key for Final Exam 153

Did You Know Statements
for Chapters 1-14. 154

Salon Fundamentals™ *Esthetics*

A SPECIAL NOTE TO STUDENTS

Would you like to guarantee success on the Esthetics Licensure Exam? If you would, here are a few common test-taking strategies that will help you improve your score on important tests.

Before the Test

Start Your Review Early

Preparation for the Esthetics Licensure Exam begins the first day of class. Students who take careful notes during class and review those notes regularly are more likely to be successful on the licensure exam.

Learn as Much as You Can About the Exam

Knowing in advance what will be covered on the exam is critical. Ask your teacher to help you determine what will be tested and begin to strengthen your understanding of this information well before you study for the exam.

Make a Study Review Guide

Making a study review guide will condense test material into a manageable size for study. Creating your own study aids such as SmartNotes™, advance organizers, chapter outlines and study briefs will help you summarize what you need to know for the test.

Organize a Study Group

Studying in a study group combines everyone's resources and usually results in higher test scores. Organizing a study group to study together well in advance of the test gives you the opportunity to share notes and discuss what will be on the test. Note: Avoid study groups that are not serious about doing well on the test.

Take Practice Tests Often

Taking a "mock test" increases confidence and builds test tolerance. Simulated tests will help you feel exactly what the licensure test situation will be like. Practice tests will also help you identify what you know and what you need to spend more time learning.

During the Test

Reduce Your Anxiety

Arrive early and relax. It is important to monitor and control your anxiety. Everyone is a little nervous when they take a test. Trust your preparation and remember that some questions will be more difficult than others. Trying to get every question correct will unnecessarily increase your anxiety and cause you to get easy questions wrong. Your goal should be to get as many questions correct as possible.

Preview the Test

Preview the entire test before you answer anything. A quick preview will help take the mystery out of the test. During your preview, note the length of the test and the types of questions you will be required to answer. Make notes to yourself about anything you think you might forget.

Read All Directions Carefully

Listen to instructions and read the directions for each section carefully. Following the directions of a test is one of the most important test-taking skills. Jumping right into the test without reading the directions carefully is often a costly mistake.

Answer Easy Questions First

Answer the questions you are sure about first. Keeping a steady pace is a very important test-taking strategy. If you answer questions in order, there is a tendency to linger too long on the difficult questions. This wastes your mental energy and usually results in a score that is lower than your ability. A better strategy is to answer the "sure thing" questions first and then come back to more difficult questions. Also, sometimes the easy questions will provide clues for answering the more difficult questions.

Figure Out Difficult Questions

Circle keywords and key points in difficult questions. This test-taking strategy will help you focus on the most important part of the question. It is also a good practice to try to rephrase difficult questions in your own words. When you return to a difficult question, think about the question, not how you are doing. Thinking about how you are doing may result in a lower score.

Salon Fundamentals™ Esthetics

Special Tips for Multiple Choice Test Questions

Read each question with the intention of answering without the help of the options provided.

If you know the answer or quickly recognize it from the options provided, answer the question. Answer all questions that you are sure of first.

If you are unsure of an answer but you can eliminate two incorrect options, you should mark this question with a check mark and return to these questions on your second pass through the test.

If you do not know the answer and cannot eliminate choices, mark the question with an "X." Return to these questions after you have answered all the questions marked with a check.

On your third pass through the questions, you should guess the answers. For questions marked with an "X," it is good practice to guess the longer and more descriptive options. If the answer to the question involves numbers, choose a number in the middle range rather than the extremes. Also, do not pay attention to answer response patterns.

You should never leave a question unanswered. Unless otherwise stated, most standardized tests do not have a penalty for guessing.

After the Test

Learn From Every Test

Reflect upon and record what you knew and what you still need to learn. Not all students are predicted to pass a licensure exam the first time. Record your thoughts about the test and learn as much as you can about the nature of the test. Thinking about how to improve in the future will eventually result in success.

A Final Note:

Test results are not intended to predict our success in life. They can, however, determine whether we have mastered the knowledge and skills necessary to become professional estheticians.

If you make a personal commitment to pass the licensure exam, prepare in advance by working with your teacher and practicing these test-taking strategies. This will greatly increase your chances for success!

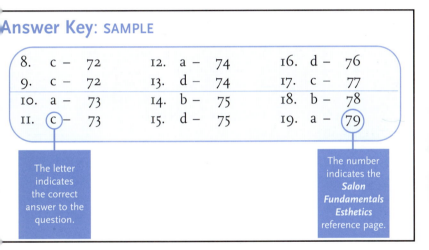

Good Luck!

There are answer keys in the back of this book to correspond with each chapter test. In the first column of the Answer Key you will find the answers, and the second column you will find the *Salon Fundamentals™ Esthetics* page references so you can locate the answers. In addition, a summary and checklist appears after the Answer Keys, called "Did You Know?" In this section, the key points are summarized based specifically on important points covered in each question.

CHAPTER 1 — Personal Development

1. The average number of hours of sleep needed per night to function properly is:
   a. two to three hours
   b. four to five hours
   c. six to eight hours
   d. nine to eleven hours

2. The body's vitality is depleted by:
   a. listening to music
   b. stress management
   c. a pleasing personality
   d. overexertion and lack of sleep

3. Cardiorespiratory activities, strength training and flexibility are part of:
   a. nutrition
   b. skin care and makeup
   c. nonverbal communication
   d. a well-balanced exercise routine

4. Stress can be managed effectively by:
   a. avoiding stress at all costs
   b. maintaining moderation and balance
   c. giving full attention to all stressful situations
   d. becoming aggressive, assertive or outspoken

5. Anger can cause the heart rate to:
   a. stop
   b. increase
   c. decrease
   d. stay the same

6. What does RDA refer to?
   a. Required Dairy Allotment
   b. Requested Dental Appointment
   c. Required Diet Association
   d. Recommended Dietary Allowances

7. The energy contained in food is measured in:
   a. degrees
   b. calories
   c. fat content
   d. protein content

8. What energy-producing substances are contained in almost all foods?
   a. nutrition, exercise and rest
   b. calories, proteins and water
   c. minerals, proteins and calories
   d. carbohydrates, proteins and fats

9. Which of the following should account for the greatest percentage of your daily nutrient intake?
   a. fats
   b. water
   c. proteins
   d. carbohydrates

10. Other essential nutrients the body needs include:
    a. nuts, seeds and legumes
    b. saturated fats and vitamins
    c. cholesterol, milk and bread
    d. water, vitamins and minerals

11. The applied science that deals with healthful living is:
    a. hygiene
    b. ergonomics
    c. microbiology
    d. communication

12. Promoting and preserving the health of the community is referred to as:
    a. public hygiene
    b. public maintenance
    c. personal hygiene
    d. personal maintenance

13. Bathing regularly with soap and using deodorant are examples of:
    a. public health
    b. public hygiene
    c. personal hygiene
    d. personal imaging

14. **Halitosis refers to:**
    a. bad breath
    b. poor posture
    c. poor nutrition
    d. poor public hygiene

15. **To maintain healthy teeth and gums and to prevent bad breath, it is necessary to practice:**
    a. oral hygiene
    b. public hygiene
    c. public sanitation
    d. stress management

16. **The nails of an esthetician should be attractively manicured and:**
    a. long
    b. short
    c. artificial
    d. polished

17. **Body support and balance are results of good posture and wearing:**
    a. tennis shoes
    b. high-heeled shoes
    c. old, comfortable, stretched-out shoes
    d. properly fitted, low, broad-heeled shoes

18. **Usually the best choice of clothing for an esthetician is:**
    a. tight-fitting
    b. simplistic
    c. trendy styles
    d. wrinkled and soiled

19. **Good posture reduces fatigue and:**
    a. causes muscle strain
    b. makes you look tired
    c. conveys low self-confidence
    d. helps internal organs function properly

20. The science that studies relationships between people and their work environment is:
    a. nutrition
    b. hygiene
    c. podiatry
    d. ergonomics

21. Varicose veins refers to:
    a. closed veins
    b. swollen veins
    c. arterial veins
    d. shriveled veins

22. A condition that numbs and weakens the hands and can eventually affect the ability to work is called:
    a. bursitis
    b. dermatitis
    c. ruptured disc
    d. Carpal Tunnel Syndrome

23. When sitting in a chair, it is important to:
    a. keep feet apart
    b. keep knees apart
    c. sit forward in the chair
    d. keep your back straight

24. The act of exchanging messages without speaking is:
    a. grammar
    b. verbal communication
    c. two-way communication
    d. nonverbal communication

25. The level and tone of voice, inflection and rate of speech all play an important role in:
    a. attitude
    b. personality
    c. verbal communication
    d. nonverbal communication

26. **Intended messages may be unclear with the use of:**
    a. tact
    b. eye contact
    c. poor grammar
    d. a pleasant voice

27. **Handling clients with tact is:**
    a. offensive to the client
    b. detrimental to the client's confidence in the esthetician
    c. not important in building professional relationships
    d. very important in building professional relationships

28. **Active listening involves:**
    a. the whole body
    b. repeating back word for word
    c. confirming verbally what was said
    d. discussing controversial topics with the clients

29. **The act of repeating out loud what was heard, processed and reported is referred to as:**
    a. active listening
    b. reflective listening
    c. whole body listening
    d. nonverbal communication

30. **A suggested topic of conversation with a client is:**
    a. politics
    b. religion
    c. controversial topics
    d. the client's lifestyle and beauty needs

31. **An esthetician should handle a complaint:**
    a. quickly and sternly
    b. calmly and judiciously
    c. by changing the topic
    d. over a long period of time

32. The outward reflection of inner feelings, thoughts, attitudes and values defines:
    a. posture
    b. hygiene
    c. personality
    d. a sense of humor

33. Friendliness, a positive attitude and vitality are all part of:
    a. habits
    b. posture
    c. a pleasing personality
    d. nonverbal communication

34. An attitude is a feeling or emotion and:
    a. can be changed
    b. is easily changed
    c. cannot be changed
    d. is impossible to identify

35. Learned behaviors that are reinforced through events in the environment are:
    a. habits
    b. moods
    c. attitudes
    d. body functions

CHAPTER 2 — Professional Development

1. A one- or two-page outline that describes personal and professional attributes in a brief, concise manner is called a:
   a. display
   b. resumé
   c. cover letter
   d. performance review

2. What type of paper is recommended for a resumé?
   a. all shades of red
   b. light pink, gray or light blue
   c. dark gray, beige or dark blue
   d. white, ivory, pale blue or pale gray

3. Professional resumé writers recommend using a font that is:
   a. 3 to 5 point
   b. 7 to 9 point
   c. 10 to 11 point
   d. 13 to 14 point

4. A necessary companion piece to the resumé that introduces you to the prospective employer is a:
   a. cover letter
   b. job interview
   c. business card
   d. performance review

5. Which of the following would present a professional image at a job interview?
   a. flashy styles
   b. excess jewelry
   c. open-toed shoes
   d. simply styled hair

6. Of the following, which is considered to be the least important factor in deciding whether to accept a position?
   a. the location
   b. the salary and benefits
   c. the size of the skin care center
   d. the success of the skin care center

7. A common practice with new employees is:
   a. gossiping about new co-workers
   b. arriving to work five minutes late
   c. changing the rules of the skin care center
   d. completing a general orientation program

8. Developing relationships with individuals who can make contact with potential customers or employers is called:
   a. retailing
   b. networking
   c. communication
   d. correspondence

9. Personal attention to the needs of the client is described as:
   a. networking
   b. communication
   c. customer service
   d. customer confidence

10. The most effective form of advertising is:
    a. direct mail
    b. newspaper ads
    c. word-of-mouth
    d. web page banners

11. An effective technique for building clientele is:
    a. gossiping about other clients
    b. pointing out the weaknesses of other stylists
    c. promoting services not offered by the skin care center
    d. asking clients to rebook before they leave the skin care center

12. Recommending and providing the best products for client purchase is called:
    a. retailing
    b. marketing
    c. networking
    d. common goals

13. Successful estheticians effectively prescribe their services along with:
    a. only inexpensive products
    b. the most expensive product in the salon
    c. the most popular product in the industry
    d. the appropriate skin care products for home care

14. The size of a product's container, the aroma or a specific ingredient of the product are its:
    a. benefits
    b. features
    c. promotions
    d. market trends

15. What a product will do to enhance the appearance or improve the condition of the client's skin are the product's:
    a. features
    b. benefits
    c. promotions
    d. common goals

16. Recommending a product that complements another product the client has already purchased is called:
    a. rebooking
    b. cross-selling
    c. correspondence
    d. sales promotion

17. To determine the continued effectiveness of recommended products and home care, the esthetician should:
    a. avoid filling out a Client Consultation Form
    b. examine the client's skin condition regularly
    c. trust the client to continue product use as directed
    d. ask the client to return only if they experience problems with the product

18. Which of the following buyer motivations is often the easiest to recognize?
    a. need
    b. profit
    c. desire
    d. impulse

19. Displaying a minimum of two products on the front edge of a display shelf creating easy access and high visibility of the products is called:
    a. end capping
    b. facing the product
    c. pricing retail products
    d. maintaining inventory control

20. The practice of visiting competitors to compare their business practices to your own is called:
    a. record keeping
    b. sales promotions
    c. guest appearances
    d. comparison shopping

CHAPTER 3 — Business Basics

1. **The central company document that the owner and employees use to make decisions is a:**
   a. self-appraisal
   b. business plan
   c. promotion calendar
   d. personal financial statement

2. **The three basic elements of a personal financial statement are:**
   a. assets, finances and exit plans
   b. assets, liabilities and net worth
   c. assets, net worth and company goals
   d. liabilities, business plans and net worth

3. **On a personal financial statement, all the money owed is called:**
   a. assets
   b. net gain
   c. net worth
   d. liabilities

4. **Assets minus liabilities equals:**
   a. assets
   b. finances
   c. net worth
   d. market need

5. **A business owned by one person who is in complete control is called a:**
   a. franchise
   b. corporation
   c. partnership
   d. sole proprietorship

6. **A business owned by two or more persons is a:**
   a. franchise
   b. corporation
   c. partnership
   d. sole proprietorship

7. Which type of business is owned by shareholders?
   a. franchise
   b. partnership
   c. corporation
   d. sole proprietorship

8. A financial advisor who sets up a basic bookkeeping system and reviews rental agreements is a(n):
   a. lawyer
   b. franchise
   c. accountant
   d. distributor sales consultant

9. An advisor on borrowing money, signing rental agreements and assuming tax responsibilities is a(n):
   a. lawyer
   b. distributor
   c. stockholder
   d. insurance agent

10. Which of the following experts acts as a link between the manufacturer and the skin care center?
    a. lawyer
    b. accountant
    c. distributor
    d. insurance agent

11. The most important factor in opening a skin care business is:
    a. finances
    b. location
    c. market need
    d. improvement costs

12. Which of the following is the first step in gauging the market need?
    a. obtaining a 10-year forecast of the economic future
    b. finding out what services other skin care centers offer
    c. finding out what type of potential clientele are in the area
    d. determining how many skin care centers are in the area

13. Which of the following measurements per esthetician allows for an efficient working space?
    a. 50 to 60 square feet
    b. 70 to 80 square feet
    c. 90 to 100 square feet
    d. 120 to 150 square feet

14. The reservoir of cash that is needed to stay ahead of creditors is called:
    a. net worth
    b. total liabilities
    c. operating capital
    d. improvement costs

15. A reserve of cash that you can draw upon to meet operating expenses if you have a slow month or two is called:
    a. liabilities
    b. line of credit
    c. Social Security
    d. operating capital

16. Which type of rent allows owners to predict monthly expenses carefully?
    a. fixed rent
    b. variable rent
    c. product liability
    d. property or premise

17. A set dollar amount paid per month plus a percentage of the total monthly income is called:
    a. fixed rent
    b. commission
    c. variable rent
    d. worker's compensation

18. Insurance is a type of:
    a. advertising
    b. commission
    c. product control
    d. risk management

19. Which type of insurance covers the cost of a lawsuit or settlement resulting from damage inflicted on a client during any service?
    a. premise
    b. property
    c. malpractice
    d. worker's compensation

20. An insurance policy that covers the actual skin care center equipment and physical location is known as:
    a. property
    b. malpractice
    c. product liability
    d. worker's compensation

21. Which of the following insurance policies is required by law?
    a. premise
    b. property
    c. malpractice
    d. worker's compensation

22. All payments received from a client for services performed and home care products purchased are referred to as:
    a. income
    b. net loss
    c. liabilities
    d. expenses

23. All costs incurred in the day-to-day running of the skin care center are called the:
    a. assets
    b. revenue
    c. net worth
    d. operating expenses

24. Utilities, supplies, cost of promotions, postage and taxes are types of:
    a. fixed costs
    b. premise costs
    c. variable costs
    d. malpractice costs

25. If the skin care center's income is greater than the operating expenses, the skin care center is operating at a(n):
    a. loss
    b. profit
    c. expense
    d. projection

26. An estimate of what will be earned in revenues and what will be paid out in expenses is called a:
    a. profit
    b. projection
    c. self-appraisal
    d. business plan

27. A withholding tax that is a planned savings/retirement fund for every worker in the United States is called:
    a. sales tax
    b. income tax
    c. property tax
    d. Social Security tax

28. Which of the following items does a skin care center owner apply for before collecting tax on products or services sold?
    a. I-9 form
    b. W-9 form
    c. resale certificate
    d. State Sales Tax Permit

29. A skin care center should keep all records of daily sales and services for at least:
    a. one week
    b. six months
    c. nine months
    d. one year

30. What type of compensation is based on a percentage of the income an individual esthetician generates?
    a. salary
    b. fixed salary
    c. commission
    d. partnership

CHAPTER 4 — Skin Care Center Ecology

1. The study of small living organisms called microbes is called:
   a. science
   b. ecology
   c. bacteriology
   d. microbiology

2. One-celled microorganisms that are classified as either disease-producing or nondisease-producing are called:
   a. virus
   b. bacteria
   c. parasites
   d. immunity

3. Nondisease-producing bacteria are called:
   a. virus
   b. microbes
   c. pathogenic bacteria
   d. nonpathogenic bacteria

4. Nonpathogenic bacteria that live on dead matter are known as:
   a. cocci
   b. bacilli
   c. spirilla
   d. saprophytes

5. Spherical or round-shaped bacterial cells that appear singularly or in groups are called:
   a. cocci
   b. bacilli
   c. spirilla
   d. saprophytes

6. Which of the following are pus-forming bacterial cells that are present in abscesses, pustules and boils?
   a. spirilla
   b. diplococci
   c. streptococci
   d. staphylococci

7. Bacterial cells that grow in pairs and cause pneumonia are known as:
   a. bacilli
   b. diplococci
   c. streptococci
   d. staphylococci

8. Which of the following is the most common form of bacterial cells?
   a. spirilla
   b. bacilli
   c. diplococci
   d. staphylococci

9. During which stage of the growth cycle do bacteria reproduce and grow rapidly?
   a. active stage
   b. inactive stage
   c. dormant stage
   d. spore-forming stage

10. The dormant stage that bacteria enter when the environment makes the bacteria's survival difficult is called the:
    a. local stage
    b. active stage
    c. inactive stage
    d. vegetative stage

11. Bacilli and spirilla are able to move themselves by using hair-like projections known as:
    a. waves
    b. spores
    c. flagella
    d. protectorates

12. A sub-microscopic infectious agent that replicates itself only within cells of living hosts is called a:
    a. cilia
    b. virus
    c. flagella
    d. parasite

13. Which of the following is a highly infectious disease that affects the liver?
    a. HIV
    b. HBV
    c. AIDS
    d. PSW

14. A highly infectious disease that interferes with the body's natural immune system is known as:
    a. listeria
    b. influenza
    c. Hepatitis B Virus (HBV)
    d. Acquired Immunodeficiency Syndrome (AIDS)

15. Head lice, itch mites, ringworm and nail fungus are all diseases caused by:
    a. infection
    b. internal parasites
    c. external parasites
    d. bloodborne pathogens

16. The growth of a parasitic organism within the body is known as a(n):
    a. infection
    b. external parasite
    c. bloodborne pathogen
    d. contaminated parasite

17. Bacteria or viruses that are transmitted through blood or body fluids and cause infectious diseases are called:
    a. airborne pathogens
    b. bloodborne pathogens
    c. airborne contaminants
    d. bloodborne contaminants

18. A contagious, potentially fatal infection caused by airborne bacteria that first affects the lungs is called:
    a. AIDS
    b. Hepatitis B
    c. chickenpox
    d. tuberculosis

19. A contagious disease refers to a disease that is:
    a. vaccinated
    b. immunized
    c. not spread from one person to another
    d. easily spread from one person to another

20. An infection present in a small, confined area indicated by a pus-filled boil, pimple or inflammation is a:
    a. local infection
    b. natural infection
    c. general infection
    d. passive infection

21. All of the following are examples of a local infection EXCEPT:
    a. boil
    b. pimple
    c. influenza
    d. inflammation

22. The body's ability to destroy infectious agents that enter it is called:
    a. immunity
    b. inflammation
    c. local infection
    d. general infection

23. The stimulation of the body's immune response through the injection of antigens is:
    a. active immunity
    b. natural immunity
    c. parasitic immunity
    d. passive immunity

24. Efforts to prevent the spread of disease and kill microbes are referred to as:
    a. infection control
    b. passive immunity
    c. cross-contamination
    d. extraction procedures

25. Infection control procedures are divided into which of the following three levels?
    a. prevention, inoculation and billing
    b. bacteriology, ecology and first aid
    c. contamination, immunity and embedded
    d. sanitation, disinfection and sterilization

26. All of the following could indicate an allergic reaction to latex EXCEPT:
    a. hives
    b. itching
    c. swelling
    d. virus

27. Sanitation is the lowest level of:
    a. sterilization
    b. contamination
    c. general infection
    d. infection control

28. Products used to arrest or prevent the growth of microorganisms on the skin are called:
    a. fungicides
    b. antiseptics
    c. bactericides
    d. disinfectants

29. Required labels on all disinfectants that inform the user about what organisms the product is effective against are called:
    a. directions
    b. bar codes
    c. brand names
    d. efficacy labels

30. Washing your hands with a liquid antibacterial soap and water is an example of procedures used during:
    a. sanitation
    b. disinfection
    c. sterilization
    d. contamination

31. The second level of infection that does not eliminate bacterial spores is called:
    a. efficacy
    b. sanitation
    c. disinfection
    d. contamination

32. Instruments can be pre-cleaned using:
    a. extracting
    b. emersing
    c. low-frequency energy waves
    d. high-frequency energy waves

33. The 2001 OSHA Bloodborne Pathogens Standard requires the use of:
    a. bar soap
    b. sanitation labels
    c. non-corrosive cleaners
    d. an EPA-registered disinfectant

34. The regulating agency that enforces safety and health standards in the workplace is:
    a. FDA
    b. DNR
    c. USDA
    d. OSHA

35. Key information proving helpful during an allergic reaction related to product usage can be found on the:
    a. EPA
    b. PSW
    c. OSHA
    d. MSDS

36. All of the information listed below could be found on a Material Safety Data Sheet (MSDS) EXCEPT:
    a. product combustion levels
    b. product pricing requirements
    c. product storage requirements
    d. hazards associated with products

37. Which of the following are porous products used in the skin care center that CANNOT be properly disinfected?
    a. lancets and tweezers
    b. probes and extractors
    c. tweezers and extractors
    d. sponges and disposable files

38. Which of the following describes the type of container required for storage of disinfected implements?
    a. moist
    b. covered
    c. uncovered
    d. contaminated

39. The process referred to as "double-bagging" is performed when a(n):
    a. antiseptic is used
    b. calibration occurs
    c. MSDS is consulted
    d. blood spill occurs

40. To protect your skin when mixing chemical disinfecting agents it is important to:
    a. wear gloves
    b. wash hands with bar soap
    c. refer to the USDA guidelines
    d. store the agents in warm, moist areas

41. The level of infection control that destroys all small organisms, including bacterial spores is called:
    a. immunity
    b. sanitation
    c. disinfection
    d. sterilization

42. Tools and instruments used to puncture or invade the skin must be sterilized or:
    a. sanitized
    b. disinfected
    c. immunized
    d. disposable

43. Which of the following machines uses UV light to kill bacteria in a dry setting?
    a. steam autoclave
    b. ultrasonic cleaner
    c. UV light sterilizer
    d. high-pressure chemiclave

44. A machine that uses pressurized steam to sterilize critical implements is referred to as a(n):
    a. UV light sanitizer
    b. UV light sterilizer
    c. steam autoclave
    d. ultrasonic cleaner

45. A machine that sterilizes surgical instruments with high-pressure, high-temperature vapor is called a(n):
    a. autoclave
    b. chemiclave
    c. UV light sterilizer
    d. ultrasonic cleaner

46. A bleeding wound should be treated by:
    a. applying a tourniquet
    b. applying hot water to the wound
    c. covering the wound and applying pressure
    d. applying a cold water compress to the wound

47. Which type of burn is usually the result of faulty equipment or improper use of equipment?
    a. heat burn
    b. exfoliant burn
    c. chemical burn
    d. electrical burn

48. What is the first course of action taken if it is suspected that a client is choking?
    a. make a thumbless fist with one hand
    b. determine if the victim can talk or cough
    c. wrap your arms around the victim's stomach
    d. perform an upward thrust by pulling the client quickly toward you

49. If a fainting victim does not regain consciousness immediately, the esthetician should:
    a. call 9-1-1
    b. roll the victim over
    c. leave the victim to rest
    d. apply a cold compress to the victim's face

50. All of the following are steps to be taken in the event of a cut, scratch or embedded object eye injury EXCEPT:
    a. try to remove embedded object
    b. place gauze pad or cloth over both eyes
    c. secure gauze pad or cloth with a bandage
    d. get to an eye specialist or emergency room immediately

CHAPTER 5 — Anatomy

1. The study of the organs and systems of the body is called:
   a. anatomy
   b. osteology
   c. physiology
   d. ergonomics

2. Which of the following is NOT part of the basic structure of a cell?
   a. tissue
   b. nucleus
   c. cytoplasm
   d. cell membrane

3. The basic units of life are:
   a. cells
   b. tissues
   c. organs
   d. systems

4. Which of the following is the control center of cell activities?
   a. nucleus
   b. cytoplasm
   c. protoplasm
   d. cell membrane

5. The production department of the cell is known as the:
   a. nucleus
   b. cytoplasm
   c. protoplasm
   d. cell membrane

6. Human cells reproduce by a process referred to as:
   a. mitosis
   b. anabolism
   c. catabolism
   d. metabolism

7. The chemical process by which cells receive nutrients for cell growth and reproduction is known as:
   a. osteology
   b. cell division
   c. metabolism
   d. indirect division

8. The process of building up larger molecules from smaller ones is:
   a. mitosis
   b. neurology
   c. expansion
   d. anabolism

9. What phase of metabolism causes a release of energy within the cell?
   a. mitosis
   b. anabolism
   c. catabolism
   d. indirect division

10. Groups of cells of the same kind make up:
    a. bones
    b. organs
    c. glands
    d. tissues

11. The tissue that carries messages to and from the brain and coordinates body functions is the:
    a. nerve tissue
    b. liquid tissue
    c. muscular tissue
    d. connective tissue

12. All of the following are organs of the body EXCEPT:
    a. skin
    b. brain
    c. hands
    d. stomach

13. Which type of tissue contracts, when stimulated, to produce motion?
    a. nerve
    b. epithelial
    c. muscular
    d. connective

14. Separate body structures that perform specific functions are:
    a. cells
    b. organs
    c. tissues
    d. systems

15. A group of body organs that perform one or more vital functions for the body is called a(n):
    a. cell
    b. organ
    c. tissue
    d. system

16. Which of the following is NOT a body system?
    a. nervous system
    b. digestive system
    c. cytoplasm system
    d. circulatory system

17. The physical foundation of the body is called the:
    a. skeletal system
    b. nervous system
    c. muscular system
    d. circulatory system

18. Osteology is the study of:
    a. bones
    b. organs
    c. muscles
    d. digestion

19. Plate-shaped bones located in the skull are:
    a. long bones
    b. flat bones
    c. irregular bones
    d. circular bones

20. The facial skeleton that encloses and protects the brain and primary sensory organs is called the:
    a. ribs
    b. ulna
    c. skull
    d. décolleté

21. The bone that extends from the top of the eyes to the top of the head to form the forehead is called the:
    a. frontal
    b. ethmoid
    c. occipital
    d. sphenoid

22. The two bones that form the crown and upper sides of the head are called:
    a. nasal bones
    b. carpal bones
    c. vomer bones
    d. parietal bones

23. How many of the 14 bones that compose the facial skeleton are involved in facial massage?
    a. 4
    b. 6
    c. 9
    d. 14

24. The lower jaw and the largest bone of the facial skeleton is the:
    a. vomer
    b. lacrimal
    c. maxillae
    d. mandible

25. The seven bones that form the top part of the spinal column are known as the:
    a. scapula
    b. turbinal bones
    c. thoracic vertebrae
    d. cervical vertebrae

26. The spine, the sternum and 12 ribs make up the:
    a. thorax
    b. humerus
    c. décolleté
    d. thoracic vertebrae

27. What are the 14 bones that form the fingers called?
    a. ulnas
    b. carpals
    c. phalanges
    d. metacarpals

28. What term is used to describe a muscle's function that means "to lift up?"
    a. levator
    b. anterior
    c. inferioris
    d. depressor

29. Which of the following is NOT a type of muscle tissue?
    a. cardiac
    b. myology
    c. voluntary
    d. involuntary

30. Which muscles respond to conscious commands?
    a. cardiac
    b. voluntary
    c. involuntary
    d. non-striated

31. The muscles that respond automatically to control various body functions are:
    a. anterior
    b. striated
    c. voluntary
    d. non-striated

32. The three parts of a muscle are the:
    a. belly, tendon and levator
    b. origin, belly and insertion
    c. insertion, ligament and dilator
    d. superioris, contraction and belly

33. The bands of fibrous tissue that attach the muscle to the bones are:
    a. organs
    b. systems
    c. tendons
    d. ligaments

34. Muscles affected by massage are generally manipulated from the:
    a. origin to the insertion
    b. insertion to the origin
    c. anterior to the posterior
    d. insertion to the posterior

35. The scalp is covered by a broad muscle called the:
    a. procerus
    b. masseter
    c. temporalis
    d. epicranius

36. What muscle is located at the nape of the neck and draws the scalp back?
    a. frontalis
    b. mentalis
    c. occipitalis
    d. aponeurosis

37. Which muscle draws brows down and wrinkles the area across the bridge of the nose?
    a. procerus
    b. corrugator
    c. oribicularis oculi
    d. levator palpebrae

38. What muscle is located outside the corners of the mouth and draws the mouth up and back, as in laughing?
    a. caninus
    b. buccinator
    c. triangularis
    d. zygomaticus

39. The muscle responsible for compressing the cheek to release air outwardly is the:
    a. risorius
    b. buccinator
    c. oris orbicularis
    d. quadratus labii superioris

40. The mastication muscle that is located above and in front of the ear and both opens and closes the jaw is the:
    a. masseter
    b. platysma
    c. trapezius
    d. temporalis

41. What muscle causes the head to move from side to side and up and down?
    a. platysma
    b. trapezius
    c. latissimus dorsi
    d. sternocleido mastoideus

42. The muscle that turns the palm of the hand up is the:
    a. tricep
    b. deltoid
    c. pronator
    d. supinator

43. The muscle located mid-forearm that bends the wrist and closes the fingers is the:
    a. bicep
    b. flexor ulnaris
    c. extensor radialis
    d. serratus anterior

44. Which hand muscles separate the fingers?
    a. adductor
    b. abductor
    c. opponens
    d. phalanges

45. The muscles that cause the thumb to move toward the fingers, giving the ability to grasp or make a fist are the:
    a. carpals
    b. adductor
    c. opponens
    d. metacarpals

46. The system that controls the circulation of the blood and lymph through the body is called the:
    a. nervous system
    b. excretory system
    c. endocrine system
    d. circulatory system

47. The heart, arteries, veins and capillaries are all part of the:
    a. muscular system
    b. respiratory system
    c. lymph vascular system
    d. cardiovascular system

48. The heart is entirely encased in a membrane called the:
    a. left atrium
    b. pericardium
    c. right ventricle
    d. depressor septi

49. The lower chambers of the heart consist of the:
    a. right atrium and left atrium
    b. left auricle and right auricle
    c. right auricle and left ventricle
    d. right ventricle and left ventricle

50. How many times per minute does a normal heart beat?
    a. 40-50 times
    b. 60-80 times
    c. 90-100 times
    d. 110-120 times

51. Blood is transported through all of the following vessels EXCEPT:
    a. veins
    b. arteries
    c. capillaries
    d. maxillaries

52. Which cells fight bacteria and other foreign substances and increase in number when infection invades the body?
    a. lymphocytes
    b. red blood cells
    c. blood platelets
    d. white blood cells

53. The process of coagulation is started by:
    a. leucocytes
    b. hemoglobin
    c. erythrocytes
    d. thrombocytes

54. The fluid part of the blood in which red and white blood cells and blood platelets are suspended is:
    a. urea
    b. plasma
    c. lymph
    d. hemoglobin

55. The blood vessels responsible for carrying oxygenated blood away from the heart through the body are:
    a. veins
    b. ureters
    c. arteries
    d. capillaries

56. The process of blood traveling from the heart throughout the body and back to the heart is referred to as:
    a. systemic circulation
    b. pulmonary circulation
    c. cardiovascular circulation
    d. lymph vascular circulation

57. The common carotid arteries supply blood to all of the following EXCEPT:
    a. legs
    b. face
    c. neck
    d. head

58. What artery supplies blood to the brain, eyes and forehead?
    a. occipital
    b. common carotid
    c. internal carotid
    d. external carotid

59. All blood from the head, face and neck returns through two veins called the:
    a. occipital artery and internal jugular
    b. internal carotid and external carotid
    c. internal carotid and internal jugular
    d. internal jugular and external jugular

60. Wearing support hose and the correctly sized shoes can help prevent:
    a. contraction
    b. metabolism
    c. mastication
    d. varicose veins

61. The facial artery that supplies blood to the lower portion of the face is called the:
    a. external maxillary
    b. posterior auricular
    c. superficial temporal
    d. internal carotid artery

62. What acts as a barrier to infection from one part of the body to another?
    a. veins
    b. ligaments
    c. lymph nodes
    d. irregular bones

63. The system that coordinates and controls the overall operation of the human body by responding to both internal and external stimuli is the:
    a. skeletal system
    b. nervous system
    c. muscular system
    d. integumentary system

64. What controls all three subsystems of the nervous system?
    a. brain
    b. nerves
    c. processes
    d. spinal cord

65. The most vital part of the brain that contains centers that control breathing and heart function is called the:
    a. pons
    b. cerebrum
    c. cerebellum
    d. medulla oblongata

66. Primary components of the nervous system include the:
    a. stomach, liver and kidneys
    b. veins, arteries and capillaries
    c. brain, spinal cord and nerves
    d. regular, irregular and flat bones

67. Which nervous system is composed of the brain and spinal cord?
    a. pulmonary system
    b. central nervous system
    c. peripheral nervous system
    d. autonomic nervous system

68. What system carries sensory information sent to the brain by the ears, eyes, nose and tongue?
    a. cardiovascular system
    b. autonomic nervous system
    c. peripheral nervous system
    d. cerebrospinal nervous system

69. What system is responsible for all involuntary body functions?
    a. skeletal system
    b. central nervous system
    c. peripheral nervous system
    d. autonomic nervous system

70. The subsystem of the autonomic system that slows the heart rate, dilates blood vessels and lowers blood pressure is the:
    a. central nervous system
    b. sympathetic nervous system
    c. cerebrospinal nervous system
    d. parasympathetic nervous system

71. The body's state of balance is referred to as:
    a. osteology
    b. anabolism
    c. homeostasis
    d. metabolism

72. The long and short threadlike fibers extending from a nerve cell are called:
    a. axons
    b. dendrites
    c. synapses
    d. cytoplasm

73. Which of the following are responsible for sending messages in the form of nerve impulses?
    a. neurons
    b. ureters
    c. processes
    d. nerve terminals

74. The interaction of sensory and motor nerves is called a(n):
    a. catabolism
    b. anabolism
    c. reflex action
    d. hormonal imbalance

75. All of the following are types of nerves EXCEPT:
    a. motor
    b. axons
    c. sensory
    d. sensory-motor

76. Nerves that carry messages from the brain to the muscles and cause a muscle to react are called:
    a. motor nerves
    b. sensory nerves
    c. afferent nerves
    d. sensory-motor nerves

77. Large nerves that perform both sensory and motor functions are called:
    a. motor nerves
    b. mixed nerves
    c. afferent nerves
    d. efferent nerves

78. Nerve cells that react to outside stimulation by sending a sensory message to the brain are:
    a. axons
    b. dendrites
    c. receptors
    d. mucus membranes

79. The eleventh cranial nerve that controls the motion of neck muscles is the:
    a. acoustic nerve
    b. auditory nerve
    c. accessory nerve
    d. hypoglossal nerve

80. The chief sensory nerve of the face responsible for transmitting facial sensations to the brain and for controlling the muscle movements of chewing is the:
    a. optic nerve
    b. vagus nerve
    c. facial nerve
    d. trifacial nerve

81. The trifacial nerve does NOT control the sensations of the:
    a. face
    b. teeth
    c. tongue
    d. fingers

82. Which of the following is NOT a branch of the trifacial nerve?
    a. nasal
    b. maxillary
    c. ophthalmic
    d. mandibular

83. The main nerve branch to the top 1/3 of the face is the:
    a. maxillary branch
    b. mandibular branch
    c. ophthalmic branch
    d. posterior auricular branch

84. What nerve extends to the side of the forehead, temple and upper part of the cheek?
    a. mental
    b. zygomatic
    c. infraorbital
    d. supra-orbital

85. The nerve that extends to the ear and to the area from the top of the head to the temple is called the:
   a. nasal
   b. mental
   c. supratrochlear
   d. auriculo temporal

86. The seventh cranial nerve and primary motor nerve of the face is called the:
   a. facial nerve
   b. trifacial nerve
   c. greater occipital nerve
   d. cervical cutaneous nerve

87. What branch of the facial nerve extends to the muscles on the side of the neck?
   a. buccal
   b. cervical
   c. mandibular
   d. posterior auricular

88. The branch of the facial nerve that extends to the muscles of the temple, the side of the forehead, the eyebrow, eyelid and upper cheek is called the:
   a. buccal
   b. digital
   c. temporal
   d. zygomatic

89. The nerve of the arm that extends down the thumb side of the arm into the back of the hand is the:
   a. ulnar
   b. radial
   c. digital
   d. median

90. What system breaks food down into simpler chemical compounds easily absorbed by cells or eliminated as waste?
    a. excretory
    b. digestive
    c. endocrine
    d. reproductive

91. All of the following are part of the digestive system EXCEPT:
    a. pharynx
    b. stomach
    c. diaphragm
    d. esophagus

92. What is secreted by the salivary glands to break down food?
    a. villi
    b. pharynx
    c. enzymes
    d. nephrons

93. The system that eliminates solid, liquid and gaseous waste products from the body is the:
    a. excretory
    b. circulatory
    c. reproductive
    d. integumentary

94. Which of the following is NOT an organ of the excretory system?
    a. skin
    b. liver
    c. lungs
    d. kidneys

95. The body's largest organ is the:
    a. skin
    b. heart
    c. brain
    d. stomach

96. What organ converts and neutralizes ammonia from the circulatory system to urea?
    a. lungs
    b. liver
    c. kidneys
    d. intestines

97. The lower respiratory tract consists of all of the following EXCEPT:
    a. lungs
    b. larynx
    c. trachea
    d. bronchi

98. A carefully balanced mechanism that directly affects hair growth, skin conditions and energy levels is the:
    a. excretory system
    b. endocrine system
    c. reproductive system
    d. integumentary system

99. The skin and its layers make up the:
    a. digestive system
    b. endocrine system
    c. reproductive system
    d. integumentary system

100. The two primary glands of the integumentary system are the sebaceous glands and which of the following?
    a. oil
    b. ductless
    c. endocrine
    d. sudoriferous

CHAPTER 6 — Electricity and Electrical Equipment

1. Light, heat, chemical and magnetic changes are all produced by:
   a. force
   b. electricity
   c. insulators
   d. a short circuit

2. The flow of electrons moving along a conductor is called a(n):
   a. rectifier
   b. hertz rating
   c. electric current
   d. circuit breaker

3. The electric current in which electrons move at an even rate and flow only in one direction is called a:
   a. load
   b. closed circuit
   c. general shock
   d. direct current

4. A rapid oscillating cycle that alternates back and forth allowing electrons to flow first in one direction and then in the other is a(n):
   a. kilowatt
   b. direct current
   c. polarity changer
   d. alternating current

5. When a generator alternates current, the number of cycles per second is called the:
   a. hertz rating
   b. ohm's rating
   c. kilowatt hours
   d. milliamperemeter

6. Material that easily transports electricity is a(n):
   a. watt
   b. prism
   c. insulator
   d. conductor

7. Materials that do not allow electricity to flow through them are called:
   a. insulators
   b. conductors
   c. open circuits
   d. closed circuits

8. Which of the following is NOT a unit of measurement for electricity?
   a. amp
   b. volt
   c. watt
   d. conductor

9. How many milliamperes equal one ampere?
   a. 10
   b. 100
   c. 1,000
   d. 1,000,000

10. A volt measures the amount of electric:
    a. pressure
    b. strength
    c. resistance
    d. frequency

11. A unit of electrical resistance is called a(n):
    a. ohm
    b. watt
    c. volt
    d. insulator

12. When electrical appliances are not in use, all of the following precautions should be taken EXCEPT:
    a. unplug the appliance
    b. turn the appliance off
    c. store appliance in a safe place
    d. submerge the appliance in water

13. A path in which electricity travels is a(n):
    a. load
    b. open circuit
    c. closed circuit
    d. grounding wire

14. What is the technical term for any appliance that requires electricity in order to work?
    a. load
    b. electron
    c. milliamp
    d. UL rating

15. More current flowing through a line than the line is designed to carry is called a(n):
    a. cathode
    b. overload
    c. spark gap
    d. power box

16. In the event of a fire that results from electrical overload you should NOT:
    a. turn off the circuit
    b. extinguish with water
    c. call the fire department if the fire is beyond your control
    d. extinguish with a fire extinguisher rated for electrical fires

17. Which of the following can occur any time a foreign conductor comes in contact with a wire carrying current to a load?
    a. short circuit
    b. iontophoresis
    c. general shock
    d. electrical shock

18. When installing a fuse do all of the following EXCEPT:
    a. wear rubber gloves
    b. turn off main power
    c. turn on all appliances
    d. unplug equipment from power source

19. Two metal pieces that make contact with each other to allow the flow of electric current are found on a(n):
    a. fuse
    b. anode
    c. circuit breaker
    d. grounding wire

20. A safety device designed to protect the user during the operation of appliances is a:
    a. load
    b. conductor
    c. power box
    d. grounding wire

21. What type of shock passes through the body and can cause burns?
    a. local shock
    b. electrocution
    c. general shock
    d. desincrustation

22. The type of shock causing the heart to stop, breathing to cease and muscles to convulse is referred to as a(n):
    a. local shock
    b. alkaline shock
    c. general shock
    d. electrotherapy shock

23. All of the following are protocols of fire prevention EXCEPT:
    a. post local fire codes
    b. inspect fire safety devices
    c. use frayed and exposed wires
    d. store flammable materials properly

24. The direct current used in electrotherapy treatments is:
    a. Tesla
    b. Faradic
    c. Galvanic
    d. Sinusoidal

25. Which type of phoresis is often used in desincrustation?
    a. Sinusoidal
    b. cataphoresis
    c. anaphoresis
    d. iontophoresis

26. Which treatment listed below uses cataphoresis to build up or nourish the deeper layers of the epidermis?
    a. phoresis
    b. anaphoresis
    c. iontophoresis
    d. desincrustation

27. Having opposite poles in an electrical current is referred to as:
    a. polarity
    b. radiation
    c. electrode
    d. Galvanic Current

28. A negatively charged electrode is called a(n):
    a. anode
    b. cathode
    c. polarity
    d. modality

29. Which of the following terms represents a positively charged electrode?
    a. load
    b. anode
    c. resistor
    d. cathode

30. When the electrode held by the esthetician is in the positive mode, the reaction on the skin will be:
    a. acidic
    b. Faradic
    c. alkaline
    d. Sinusoidal

31. Tesla, a High Frequency Current, is also known as the:
    a. red ray
    b. violet ray
    c. infrared ray
    d. ultraviolet ray

32. All of the following statements are benefits of Direct High Frequency EXCEPT:
    a. stimulates surface tissue
    b. stimulates sebum production
    c. heals existing papules and pustules
    d. increases circulation and blood flow

33. A narrow space between the electrode and the skin used to provide germicidal healing and drying effects during either Direct or Indirect High Frequency treatments is a:
    a. load
    b. converter
    c. conductor
    d. spark gap

34. Faradic Current is used chiefly to cause:
    a. soothing effects
    b. chemical effects
    c. the transfer of heat
    d. muscle contractions

35. An alternating current that penetrates more deeply and can provide greater stimulation to the treated area than a Faradic Current is called:
    a. Galvanic
    b. Sinusoidal
    c. High Frequency
    d. Indirect Faradic

36. Pregnancy, epilepsy, diabetes or other conditions that suggest it is inadvisable to perform a procedure on a client is a(n):
    a. pyrolysis
    b. UL rating
    c. thermal effect
    d. contraindication

37. A combination light that can be broken into its individual wavelengths by a prism is referred to as:
    a. white light
    b. invisible light
    c. fluorescent light
    d. incandescent light

38. Bacteria that cause skin infections can be killed by:
    a. visible light
    b. infrared light
    c. ultraviolet light
    d. incandescent light

39. Which type of ultraviolet ray is most frequently used in tanning booths?
    a. UVA rays
    b. UVB rays
    c. UVC rays
    d. UVD rays

40. The transfer of heat via direct contact is:
    a. radiation
    b. electricity
    c. convection
    d. conduction

41. What effect does a rotating brush produce?
    a. thermal
    b. heating
    c. mechanical
    d. electrochemical

42. Electric current that travels through a water-based solution and onto the body has a(n):
    a. thermal effect
    b. magnetic effect
    c. mechanical effect
    d. electrochemical effect

43. Which type of electrical equipment utilizes violet rays or black light to analyze skin type and condition?
    a. loupe
    b. Wood's Lamp
    c. magnifying lamp
    d. electric pulverizer

44. A device that sprays a lukewarm, diffused vapor mist onto the surface of the skin is called a(n):
    a. skin scope
    b. facial steamer
    c. suction machine
    d. dermascope

45. Which of the following is NOT a contraindication for using the steam machine?
    a. rosacea
    b. thick skin
    c. sensitive skin
    d. couperose skin

CHAPTER 7 — Chemistry

1. The study of the elements in the Periodic Table and their compounds except the compounds based on carbon is:
   a. chemistry
   b. biochemistry
   c. organic chemistry
   d. inorganic chemistry

2. Anything that occupies space is called:
   a. matter
   b. energy
   c. chemistry
   d. combustion

3. All of the following statements are true about liquids EXCEPT:
   a. they have definite shape
   b. they have definite weight
   c. they have definite volume
   d. they take the shape of the container in which they are poured

4. Matter with definite weight, but indefinite volume and shape are:
   a. solids
   b. gases
   c. liquids
   d. compounds

5. A change in a substance that creates a new substance with different material characteristics from those of the original substance is a:
   a. phase change
   b. physical change
   c. chemical change
   d. chemical structure

6. All of the following statements are true about physical changes EXCEPT:
   a. chemical structure does not change
   b. changes always involve either the gain or loss of energy
   c. a new substance possessing different material composition is created
   d. freezing water to form ice cubes is an example of a physical change

7. The unifying concept used to organize elements and their similarities is called the:
   a. periodic law
   b. free electron
   c. atomic number
   d. molecular weight

8. All of the following statements about the Period Table of Chemical Elements are true EXCEPT:
   a. there are 92 naturally occurring elements
   b. the atomic number is the primary basis for organization
   c. Dmitri Mendeleev and Lothar Meyer found ways of arranging elements
   d. the unifying concept used to organize elements is called scientific shorthand

9. Which of the following is the most abundant element in the earth's crust?
   a. carbon
   b. oxygen
   c. nitrogen
   d. hydrogen

10. Which of the following have a positive electrical charge and identify the atom?
    a. ions
    b. protons
    c. neutrons
    d. electrons

11. The molecular weight of each element is determined by the:
    a. protons
    b. protons and neutrons
    c. protons and electrons
    d. neutrons and electrons

12. Which of the following items have a negative electrical charge?
    a. protons
    b. neutrons
    c. electrons
    d. elements

13. Which of the following is created by chemically uniting two different elements?
    a. atom
    b. element
    c. molecule
    d. compound

14. All of the following statements about compounds are true EXCEPT:
    a. held together by chemical bonds
    b. lack unique chemical and physical characteristics
    c. formed by the union of individual elements
    d. more than four million have been identified

15. Which of the following is a process in which a substance gains an electron and oxygen is released?
    a. oxidation
    b. reduction
    c. ionic bonding
    d. covalent bonding

16. The branch of science that deals with the chemicals related to life processes and their reactions within the body is called:
    a. anatomy
    b. biochemistry
    c. organic chemistry
    d. inorganic chemistry

17. Which of the following are materials that dissolve and break down large molecules into smaller ones?
    a. lipids
    b. proteins
    c. enzymes
    d. amino acids

18. All of the following statements about amino acids are true EXCEPT:
    a. there are 22 common amino acids
    b. they join together in chains to form proteins
    c. they dissolve and break down large molecules
    d. they consist of carbon, oxygen, hydrogen and nitrogen

19. All of the following statements about carbohydrates are true EXCEPT:
    a. they play a key role in metabolism
    b. they are used by the body to store energy
    c. they are used to construct and renew the body
    d. glucose is the most important carbohydrate for providing energy

20. A simple unit of a carbohydrate is called a:
    a. saccharide
    b. disaccharide
    c. polysaccharide
    d. monosaccharide

21. Which of the following is the term used to describe a base product?
    a. acid
    b. alkaline
    c. hydrogen
    d. logarithmic

22. Which of the following is the average pH range of the skin?
    a. 2.5 to 3.5
    b. 4.5 to 5.5
    c. 6.5 to 7.5
    d. 8.5 to 9.5

23. A mixture of sebum and sweat combined with lipids, minerals and moisture to form a protective barrier for the skin is called the:
    a. base
    b. hydroxide ion
    c. acid mantle
    d. potential hydrogen

24. You can keep your clients' skin in top shape by doing all of the following EXCEPT:
    a. reading labels knowledgeably
    b. selecting and recommending the right product for home care
    c. using harsh soaps and cleansers without a toner or moisturizer
    d. treating each client with products that balance the individual's pH

25. The solid, or dissolved part, of a solution is called the:
    a. solute
    b. solvent
    c. suspension
    d. saturation point

26. The term that describes when a solute will no longer dissolve evenly in the solvent is the:
    a. suspension
    b. saturation point
    c. miscible solvent
    d. homogeneous dispersion

27. Solvents that easily mix together are called:
    a. miscible
    b. emulsions
    c. immiscible
    d. suspensions

28. A hard, low-level water or anhydrous product used by rubbing the product directly on the skin is called:
    a. stick
    b. powder
    c. aerosol
    d. emulsion

29. All of the following statements regarding aerosols are true EXCEPT:
    a. they are explosive and flammable
    b. they are products packaged under pressure
    c. they are environmentally friendly to discard
    d. they are blended with a propellant inside a container

30. Which ingredient listed below is compatible with both water and oil?
    a. fatty acid
    b. emulsifier
    c. humectant
    d. surfactant

31. Ingredients responsible for producing the desired effect are called:
    a. surfactants
    b. humectants
    c. active ingredients
    d. inactive ingredients

32. Which of the following is the first ingredient found in the majority of cosmetic skin care products?
    a. water
    b. dimethicone
    c. methylparaben
    d. cyclomethicone

33. Which of the following are organic ingredients that bind water and deposit it onto the skin?
    a. fatty acids
    b. emollients
    c. surfactants
    d. humectants

34. All of the following statements about emollients are true EXCEPT:
    a. they are used to condition and soften the skin
    b. they provide a protective barrier called an occlusive barrier
    c. they are found in concentrations ranging between 20% and 30%
    d. they help the skin maintain its natural hydration by sealing moisture in the skin

35. Which of the following have the ability to bind a wide range of organic and inorganic matter to water?
    a. emollients
    b. surfactants
    c. fatty acids
    d. humectants

36. Which of the following allow for the suspension of small particle solids in a base by creating a supporting structure to prevent settling?
    a. emollients
    b. botanicals
    c. thickeners
    d. humectants

37. All of the following are benefits that may be derived from botanicals EXCEPT:
    a. drying effects
    b. conditioning effects
    c. antibacterial effects
    d. anti-inflammatory effects

38. Which of the following are included in cosmetic products to maintain microbiological integrity or product quality during production, storage and use by the consumer?
    a. thickeners
    b. botanicals
    c. preservatives
    d. viscosity modifiers

39. Which of the following are vegetable, mineral or pigment dyes that are added to products to enhance its appearance?
    a. botanicals
    b. coloring agents
    c. chelating agents
    d. antibacterial agents

40. Which of the following means the product is less likely to provoke an allergic reaction?
    a. fragrance
    b. allergenic
    c. antibacterial
    d. hypoallergenic

41. An ingredient used in skin care products to cover (mask) undesirable odors in the product base is:
    a. water
    b. fragrance
    c. fatty alcohol
    d. hydroxy acid

42. Acids or bases used to adjust the desired product pH level are called:
    a. comedogenic
    b. pH adjustors
    c. active ingredients
    d. non-comedogenic

43. Which of the following are ingredients that are likely to block or clog the pores and contribute to pimples?
    a. antibacterial
    b. comedogenic
    c. hypoallergenic
    d. non-comedogenic

44. All of the following statements about sunscreens are true EXCEPT:
    a. they are inactive ingredients
    b. they are usually 2% to 7% in concentration
    c. they are considered drugs under FDA guidelines
    d. they are used in products to block or absorb ultraviolet radiation emitted by the sun

45. Chemically unstable molecules caused by environmental pollutants and UV exposure are called:
   a. silicones
   b. antioxidants
   c. free radicals
   d. hydroxy acids

46. Which of the following is a non-comedogenic emollient that gives products a silky feel?
   a. dimethicone
   b. hydroxy acids
   c. cyclomethicone
   d. dimethicone copolyol

47. Organic acids extracted from a variety of natural sources such as fruits, sugar and milk are called:
   a. vitamins
   b. enzymes
   c. hydroxy acids
   d. dimethicone copolyol

48. Ingredients that are designed to dissolve keratin proteins on the surface of the skin are called:
   a. vitamins
   b. enzymes
   c. lighteners
   d. coloring agents

49. All of the following statements about lighteners are true EXCEPT:
   a. they are used at relatively high levels
   b. they slowly block the production of melanin in the skin
   c. they are used to bleach or lighten areas of hyperpigmentation
   d. they usually take months of continued use to deliver a noticeable effect

50. The promotion and advertising of cosmetics and many other products are regulated by the:
   a. FDA
   b. FTC
   c. CTFA
   d. FFDCA

CHAPTER 8 — Skin Physiology

1. The study of the skin's functions is referred to as:
   a. etiology
   b. histology
   c. morphology
   d. skin physiology

2. All of the following are functions of the skin EXCEPT:
   a. secretion
   b. protection
   c. absorption
   d. excoriation

3. Tiny openings that allow sweat or sebum to pass through the surface of the skin are called:
   a. pores
   b. organs
   c. tissues
   d. follicles

4. Which of the following provides the body with its first line of defense against infection by identifying foreign substances in the skin?
   a. sweat
   b. sebum
   c. arrector pili
   d. immune cells

5. A complex mixture of fatty acids that keeps the skin soft, supple and pliable is known as:
   a. sweat
   b. keratin
   c. sebum
   d. sudoriferous

6. Which of the following is NOT one of the main layers of the skin?
   a. dermal
   b. tendon
   c. epidermal
   d. subcutaneous

7. Which of the following layers of skin is known as the protective layer?
   a. dermis
   b. epidermis
   c. stratum corneum
   d. subcutaneous layer

8. The epidermis is primarily composed of:
   a. sebum
   b. adipose
   c. desmosomes
   d. keratinocytes

9. Which of the following is the toughest layer of the epidermis?
   a. stratum lucidum
   b. stratum spinosum
   c. stratum corneum
   d. stratum germinativum

10. Keratinocytes on the surface of the skin remain tightly interconnected by intercellular connections called:
    a. whorls
    b. desmosomes
    c. squamous cells
    d. epidermal ridges

11. "Spiny" irregularly shaped cells are located in the:
    a. stratum corneum
    b. stratum spinosum
    c. stratum granulosum
    d. stratum germinativum

12. The layer of skin in which the cells are more regularly shaped and resemble many tiny granules is the:
    a. stratum corneum
    b. stratum spinosum
    c. stratum granulosum
    d. stratum germinativum

13. A strong protein substance that, when broken down, forms bundles that strengthen and give structure to the skin is:
    a. scars
    b. dermis
    c. keloids
    d. collagen

14. Which of the following is referred to as the "true skin?"
    a. dermis
    b. epidermis
    c. subdermis
    d. subcutaneous

15. Which of the following is NOT a receptor of sensation in the dermal layer of the skin?
    a. mast cells
    b. Ruffini's corpuscles
    c. Krause's end bulbs
    d. Meissner's corpuscles

16. What do sudoriferous-glands produce?
    a. blood
    b. saliva
    c. sweat
    d. sebum

17. Apocrine glands are located on all of the following parts of the body EXCEPT the:
    a. feet
    b. nipples
    c. genitals
    d. underarm area

18. Eccrine glands are most abundant in all of the following areas EXCEPT the:
    a. forehead
    b. underarm area
    c. soles of the feet
    d. palms of the hands

19. What is the male hormone that influences the production of sebum?
    a. androgen
    b. acid mantle
    c. exocrine glands
    d. endocrine glands

20. What is the structure that insulates and acts as a shock absorber to protect the bones?
    a. ligaments
    b. nervous tissue
    c. epithelial tissue
    d. subcutaneous layer

21. What is the name of the connective tissue that holds bones to other bones to form joints?
    a. tendons
    b. muscles
    c. cartilage
    d. ligaments

22. Which of the following is NOT a form of tissue found in the skin?
    a. nervous
    b. muscular
    c. connective
    d. keratinocytes

23. Which of the following is NOT a type of sensory cell?
    a. microphages
    b. pain receptors
    c. thermoreceptors
    d. Pacinian corpuscles

24. The removal of dead skin that stimulates new cell growth is called:
    a. dermal
    b. exfoliation
    c. transdermal
    d. sun exposure

25. All of the following are factors of skin absorption EXCEPT:
    a. hair follicles
    b. hydration level
    c. oiliness of the skin
    d. temperature of the skin

26. Which of the following refers to a change in the structure of the skin tissue?
    a. lesion
    b. eczema
    c. erythema
    d. dermatitis

27. Which secondary lesion is a dried mass that is the remains of an oozing sore?
    a. scar
    b. scale
    c. crust
    d. fissure

28. A hereditary rash, or an inflammation of the skin, characterized by dry, sensitive, irritated skin is called a(n):
    a. macule
    b. atopic dermatitis
    c. contact dermatitis
    d. seborrheic dermatitis

29. An allergic reaction that produces an eruption of wheals is known as:
    a. hives
    b. eczema
    c. infection
    d. psoriasis

30. Which of the following is a highly contagious viral infection that causes an eruptive, blister-like cluster?
    a. shingles
    b. psoriasis
    c. Herpes Zoster
    d. Herpes Simplex

31. Warts are most commonly found on the following areas of the body EXCEPT the:
    a. feet
    b. legs
    c. hands
    d. fingers

32. A chronic inflammatory condition of the face in which the small capillaries of the face become dilated and inflamed is called:
    a. acne
    b. milia
    c. rosacea
    d. whiteheads

33. Acne can be caused by all of the following EXCEPT:
    a. genetics
    b. emotional stress
    c. hormonal changes
    d. eating too much chocolate

34. What is another name for a whitehead?
    a. acne
    b. open comedo
    c. closed comedo
    d. propionibacterium

35. Which of the following is NOT a myth of acne?
    a. acne can be cleared up
    b. acne must just run its course
    c. acne is caused by a poor diet
    d. acne is caused by poor hygiene

36. Which of the following is an ingredient used to dry, exfoliate and help in killing bacteria?
    a. Metrogel
    b. androgen
    c. Vitamin C
    d. benzoyl peroxide

37. A foul smelling perspiration caused by the yeast and bacteria that break down the sweat on the surface of the skin is called:
    a. anihidrosis
    b. bromidrosis
    c. hyperhidrosis
    d. malaria rubra

38. Which of the following are small elevated growths that can easily be removed by a physician?
    a. skin tags
    b. leukoderma
    c. basal cell carcinomas
    d. squamous cell carcinoma

39. What is a congenital disease that results in the failure of the skin to produce melanin?
    a. vitiligo
    b. albinism
    c. leukoderma
    d. hyperpigmentation

40. A birthmark or congenital mole is called a:
    a. nevus
    b. melasma
    c. melanoma
    d. hyperpigmentation

41. A freckle is called a(n):
    a. nevus
    b. vitiligo
    c. lentigo
    d. leukoderma

Salon Fundamentals™ Esthetics

42. Which of the following is a term used to identify a rapid onset of an intense and severe condition?
    a. acute
    b. chronic
    c. prognosis
    d. contagious

43. The term used to describe symptoms that are frequent and continuing is:
    a. acute
    b edema
    c. chronic
    d. contagious

44. A swelling of tissue or skin caused by an excessive accumulation of fluid in the tissues is called:
    a. allergy
    b. edema
    c. erythema
    d. hyperkeratosis

45. Which of the following is the term for the buildup of skin cells on the epidermis?
    a. edema
    b. keratosis
    c. erythema
    d. dermatitis

46. An inflammation in the skin that causes severe itching, usually on undamaged skin, is known as:
    a. pruritus
    b. dermatitis
    c. hyperkeratosis
    d. dermatitis venenata

47. Which of the following describes a disease that is active internally throughout the body system?
    a. parasitic disease
    b. systemic disease
    c. seasonal disease
    d. subjective symptoms

48. What does intrinsic aging indicate?
    a. unnatural aging
    b. natural aging process
    c. being exposed to the sun
    d. aging affects from alcohol

49. Which of the following is the number one factor in extrinsic aging?
    a. diabetes
    b. smoking
    c. physical effects of aging
    d. amount of sun exposure

50. The general appearance of sun-damaged skin shows all of the following major structural changes EXCEPT:
    a. a leathery face
    b. irregular pigment
    c. a significant increase of elasticity
    d. numerous fine lines and wrinkles

CHAPTER 9 — Client Care

1. **All of the following are ways to greet a client professionally and respectfully EXCEPT:**
   a. offer a friendly smile
   b. avoid direct eye contact
   c. welcome the client warmly
   d. extend your hand and shake hands firmly

2. **Which element listed below is usually the first contact a client has with the skin care center?**
   a. radio ad
   b. brochure
   c. telephone
   d. newspaper

3. **The nonverbal gesture that conveys undivided attention and demonstrates personal confidence is:**
   a. touch
   b. eye contact
   c. raised eyebrow
   d. sideway glance

4. **The preferred tone of voice in professional settings is:**
   a. loud
   b. low key
   c. hesitant
   d. high-pitched

5. **Which of the following is NOT a component of the Client Consultation Form?**
   a. personal income
   b. treatment record
   c. personal skin evaluation
   d. professional skin evaluation

6. What section of the Client Consultation Form asks for basic data that can be used to offer marketing promotions?
   a. medical history
   b. treatment record
   c. personal information
   d. professional skin evaluation

7. What section of the Client Consultation Form identifies possible contraindication for particular products, equipment and services to be used or performed?
   a. medical history
   b. treatment record
   c. personal information
   d. professional skin evaluation

8. A substance or ingredient likely to cause an allergic reaction is referred to as a(n):
   a. HRT
   b. PABA
   c. allergen
   d. Accutane®

9. Allergies to alpha and beta hydroxy acids can cause:
   a. acne
   b. irritation
   c. thinning of the skin
   d. decreased sensitivity

10. Hyperpigmentation, acne and increased dryness are all possible side effects of:
    a. steroids
    b. Accutane
    c. oral antibiotics
    d. hormone replacement therapy

11. All of the following conditions should avoid treatments that utilize electrical current EXCEPT:
    a. epilepsy
    b. diabetes
    c. pregnancy
    d. pacemakers

12. Dilated capillaries that can be treated with gentle massage and soothing, mild products are referred to as:
    a. diabetes
    b. varicose veins
    c. telangiectasia
    d. thyroid conditions

13. Any types of treatments should be avoided on clients with active:
    a. telangiectasia
    b. heart conditions
    c. thyroid conditions
    d. Herpes Simplex lesions

14. Which of the following is NOT a lifestyle factor that may affect the skin?
    a. diet
    b. exercise
    c. smoking
    d. low pain threshold

15. A lifestyle factor that robs nutrients and oxygen from the skin is:
    a. diet
    b. exercise
    c. smoking
    d. proper nutritition

16. Regular exercise promotes a healthy body and skin by increasing:
    a. dryness
    b. circulation
    c. premature wrinkles
    d. clogging and comedones

17. Which of the following may protect the skin care center from claims related to damage that may occur to the client's skin as a result of the services provided?
    a. skin evaluation
    b. client treatment record
    c. client release statement
    d. client personal skin evaluation

18. The part of the Client Consultation Form in which the esthetician reviews and evaluates the skin is the:
    a. treatment record
    b. personal information
    c. personal skin evaluation
    d. professional skin evaluation

19. How often should a professional skin analysis be performed?
    a. annually
    b. only on the first visit
    c. every six months at a minimum
    d. each visit

20. Which of the following is NOT an indicator of an effective skin care treatment?
    a. decreased wrinkles
    b. improved hydration
    c. increased pore size
    d. improved pigmentation

21. The size of the pores is most visible on the:
    a. eye area
    b. chin area
    c. cheek area
    d. forehead area

Salon Fundamentals™ Esthetics

22. The key ingredient a product contains that makes it effective is referred to as the:
    a. core
    b. factor
    c. benefit
    d. feature

23. Asking the client to schedule another appointment in advance is referred to as:
    a. residual
    b. redirecting
    c. completing
    d. rebooking

24. Which of the following steps should NOT be followed upon completion of the treatment?
    a. provide clients with a home care treatment plan
    b. discredit products that the clients are currently using
    c. review with clients the products used during the treatment
    d. stress the features and benefits of recommended products

25. An explanation of what a product will do and why is called a:
    a. skin evaluation
    b. release statement
    c. product statement
    d. Client Consultation Form

26. The results that the ingredients deliver are called:
    a. labels
    b. features
    c. benefits
    d. product statement

27. What percent of service dollars does retail account for?
    a. 5% to 10%
    b. 15% to 30%
    c. 40% to 50%
    d. more than 50%

28. What percent of more new clients should you strive to acquire each week?
    a. 15% to 20%
    b. 25% to 30%
    c. 35% to 40%
    d. 45% to 50%

29. What is the best form of advertising in any customer service business?
    a. business cards
    b. word-of-mouth
    c. radio advertisements
    d. newspaper advertisements

30. What is the recommended timeline for follow-up calls and notes?
    a. within 1 week
    b. within 8 hours
    c. within 72 hours
    d. the day after the service

CHAPTER 10 — Facials

1. All of the following are elements of proper skin care that combine to result in healthy, glowing skin EXCEPT:
   a. regular exercise
   b. a well-balanced diet
   c. an adequate intake of water
   d. excessive exposure to the sun

2. How often is the basic regimen of cleansing, toning, moisturizing and protecting recommended to be followed?
   a. once daily
   b. twice daily
   c. three times daily
   d. three times weekly

3. What step in the basic skin care regimen is specifically designed to remove dirt, oil, makeup and environmental pollutants from the surface of the skin?
   a. toning
   b. cleansing
   c. protecting
   d. moisturizing

4. Which of the following is the final step of the basic skin care regimen that deals with harmful UVA and UVB rays projected from the sun?
   a. toning
   b. cleansing
   c. protecting
   d. moisturizing

5. What SPF number is recommended for sports or swimming when perspiration or water can wash away the sunscreen?
   a. 10
   b. 15
   c. 25
   d. 30

6. The most effective sunscreens contain ingredients that act as:
   a. blockers
   b. absorbers
   c. both blockers and absorbers
   d. neither blockers nor absorbers

7. Which of the following works in conjunction with other ingredients to cause a chemical reaction to remove dead skin cells?
   a. astringent
   b. sunscreen
   c. chemical exfoliant
   d. mechanical exfoliant

8. Which of the following types of masks are ideal for dry skin types?
   a. gel masks
   b. crème masks
   c. paraffin masks
   d. clay/mud masks

9. What type of mask seals the skin, locking in moisture and creating a firm, taut feeling after removal?
   a. crème mask
   b. paraffin mask
   c. clay/mud mask
   d. modeling mask

10. What type of mask increases circulation and promotes penetration of nutrients or ingredients applied underneath it?
    a. gel mask
    b. crème mask
    c. paraffin mask
    d. modeling mask

11. Which of the following is a systematic, therapeutic method of manipulating the body by rubbing, pinching, tapping, kneading or stroking?
    a. massage
    b. hydration
    c. dehydration
    d. contraindication

12. All of the following are benefits of massage EXCEPT:
    a. tighter, firmer muscles
    b. stronger muscle tissue
    c. stimulation of glandular activities of the skin
    d. decreased circulation of the blood supply to the skin

13. A light, relaxing, smooth, gentle, stroking or circular movement used in massage is known as:
    a. friction
    b. effleurage
    c. petrissage
    d. tapotement

14. Which of the following is probably the most important of the massage movements?
    a. vibration
    b. effleurage
    c. petrissage
    d. tapotement

15. Which of the following areas should NOT be stimulated by petrissage movements?
    a. eyes
    b. arms
    c. shoulders
    d. upper back

16. The massage movement that is the most stimulating and is used for the shortest period of time is:
    a. friction
    b. vibration
    c. effleurage
    d. tapotement

17. A massage motion that resembles a chopping movement using the edge of the hands is known as:
    a. fulling
    b. hacking
    c. wringing
    d. chucking

18. Which of the following is a form of friction performed by holding the client's arm in one hand and lifting the skin firmly up and down over the bone with the other hand?
    a. fulling
    b. hacking
    c. wringing
    d. chucking

19. The shaking movement achieved when the esthetician quickly shakes his or her arms while the fingertips or palms are touching the client is called:
    a. friction
    b. vibration
    c. petrissage
    d. tapotement

20. Contraindications for massage include all of the following EXCEPT:
    a. previous stroke
    b. heart conditions
    c. low blood pressure
    d. high blood pressure

21. All of the following are important points to remember about massage manipulations EXCEPT:
    a. check for contraindications first
    b. direct movements from origin to insertion
    c. provide an even tempo or rhythm and pressure
    d. practice techniques on a mannequin head or on your knee

22. Which of the following skin types displays few breakouts or clogged areas?
    a. dry
    b. oily
    c. normal
    d. combination

23. The skin type that lacks sebum production and appears thin and delicate is:
    a. dry
    b. oily
    c. normal
    d. mature/aging

24. Which of the following skin types is less likely to display fine lines and wrinkles?
    a. oily
    b. normal
    c. combination
    d. mature/aging

25. The most common skin type is:
    a. dry
    b. oily
    c. normal
    d. combination

26. All of the following are qualities of mature/aging skin EXCEPT:
    a. lack of firmness
    b. increased dryness
    c. excessive elasticity
    d. apparent fine lines and wrinkles

27. The skin condition that displays fine dilated capillaries is known as:
    a. acne
    b. oily
    c. couperose
    d. dehydration

28. Which of the following is a vascular disorder characterized by flushed redness, dilated capillaries and small red bumps?
    a. acne
    b. rosacea
    c. couperose
    d. dehydration

29. The skin condition caused by overactivity of the sebaceous glands that generally occurs during adolescence is known as:
    a. acne
    b. rosacea
    c. couperose
    d. dehydration

30. If the esthetician suspects a medical condition, he or she should:
    a. treat the condition
    b. ignore the condition
    c. offer home treatment advice to client
    d. refer the client to a dermatologist or specialist

31. Which of the following skin care products assist in cleansing the skin and returning normal to dry skin to a normal pH?
    a. antiseptic
    b. astringent
    c. manual exfoliant
    d. chemical exfoliant

32. Which of the following types of skin care equipment allows a thorough examination of the skin's surface?
    a. Wood's Lamp
    b. infrared lamp
    c. magnifying lamp
    d. multifunction machine

33. The skin care equipment that relaxes the client and softens the skin to allow for penetration of a product is called a(n):
    a. infrared lamp
    b. facial steamer
    c. magnifying lamp
    d. multifunction machine

34. Which of the following allows for superficial exfoliation and deep cleansing of the skin?
   a. vacuum
   b. Wood's Lamp
   c. facial steamer
   d. rotating brush

35. Which of the following is NOT a proper procedure for infection control and safety?
   a. store products in a warm place
   b. keep lids tightly closed on product jars
   c. discard any implements that cannot be disinfected
   d. wash and sanitize hands before and after every client

36. Which of the following is the first step in performing a basic facial?
   a. analyze the client's skin
   b. wash and sanitize hands
   c. place eye pads over the client's eyes
   d. drape client and position headband or hairnet

37. A highly alkaline solution that liquefies sebum is known as:
   a. toner
   b. Galvanic current
   c. massage crème
   d. desincrustation solution

38. Approximately how long should a mask be left to set on the face?
   a. 1 to 2 minutes
   b. 3 to 4 minutes
   c. 5 to 10 minutes
   d. 15 to 20 minutes

39. After completing a basic facial, the esthetician should do all of the following EXCEPT:
    a. offer to book the client's next visit
    b. recommend retail products to the client
    c. arrange products and implements for next service
    d. throw unused cotton pads and sponges in waste receptacle

40. The current used to amplify the effects of massage movements for relaxation and stimulation is called:
    a. Direct Low Frequency
    b. Indirect Low Frequency
    c. Direct High Frequency
    d. Indirect High Frequency

CHAPTER 11 — Hair Removal

1. All of the following are temporary hair removal procedures EXCEPT:
   a. shaving
   b. tweezing
   c. electrolysis
   d. chemical depilatories

2. Which of the following is caused by hormonal imbalances, and typically affects women by causing dark hair to grow in areas of the body such as the face, arms, legs and back?
   a. capilli
   b. hirsutism
   c. supercilia
   d. hypertrichosis

3. Excessive hair growth which is genetically determined is called:
   a. capilli
   b. hirsutism
   c. supercilia
   d. hypertrichosis

4. Which of the following is hair that grows on the scalp?
   a. cilia
   b. capilli
   c. barba
   d. lanugo

5. Thick, coarse hair that grows on the face to form a beard is called:
   a. cilia
   b. capilli
   c. barba
   d. lanugo

6. Which of the following is eyelash hair?
   a. cilia
   b. vellus
   c. capilli
   d. supercilia

7. Eyebrow hair is called:
   a. barba
   b. vellus
   c. terminal
   d. supercilia

8. Soft, downy hair on the body at birth is called:
   a. vellus
   b. lanugo
   c. terminal
   d. supercilia

9. Which of the following is thin, soft, unpigmented hair covering the body?
   a. vellus
   b. lanugo
   c. terminal
   d. supercilia

10. Which of the following is thicker, pigmented hair that grows on areas of the body after puberty?
    a. capilli
    b. lanugo
    c. terminal
    d. supercilia

11. All of the following are phases of the hair life cycle EXCEPT:
    a. telogen phase
    b. anagen phase
    c. catagen phase
    d. delivery phase

12. The first and longest phase where hair actively grows is called:
    a. telogen phase
    b. anagen phase
    c. catagen phase
    d. completion phase

13. The stage in which the hair begins to destroy itself as it disconnects from the papilla is called:
    a. telogen phase
    b. anagen phase
    c. catagen phase
    d. completion phase

14. Which of the following is the phase in which the hair sheds, and the follicle rests and prepares to resume to the anagen phase?
    a. telogen
    b. anagen
    c. catagen
    d. interphase

15. In which type of temporary hair removal technique does hair usually grow back within 24 to 48 hours?
    a. waxing
    b. shaving
    c. tweezing
    d. chemical depilatory

16. All of the following statements are true about a chemical depilatory EXCEPT:
    a. regrowth will occur within several days
    b. it removes hair by decomposing the papilla
    c. thioglycolic acid derivative is the main ingredient
    d. a patch test must be performed prior to application

17. How long are chemical depilatories generally left on the skin?
    a. 5 minutes
    b. 10 minutes
    c. 15 minutes
    d. 20 minutes

18. Which of the following chemically lightens the hair by removing pigment?
    a. wax
    b. bleach
    c. electrolysis
    d. thermolysis

19. Which of the following may be used to remove unwanted hair from smaller areas and can be very beneficial in finishing the eyebrow design?
    a. waxing
    b. shaving
    c. tweezing
    d. threading

20. The most popular waxing service in the skin care center is the:
    a. chin
    b. back
    c. upper lip
    d. bikini line

21. The majority of professional waxing services are performed with:
    a. soft wax
    b. hard wax
    c. sugar paste
    d. low-level current

22. Which of the following is ideal for small areas and thinner, more sensitive skin?
    a. soft wax
    b. strip wax
    c. hard wax
    d. classic wax

23. An ancient method of hair removal using a cotton thread is called:
    a. waxing
    b. sugaring
    c. tweezing
    d. threading

24. Which of the following is a hair removal technique that involves applying a paste to the skin in a rolling motion?
    a. sugaring
    b. tweezing
    c. threading
    d. chemical depilatory

25. How long does the sugaring method of hair removal generally last?
    a. 1 to 2 days
    b. 1 to 2 weeks
    c. 4 to 6 weeks
    d. 8 to 10 weeks

26. Which of the following is a method of hair removal that requires the technician to insert a small needle into each hair follicle?
    a. sugaring
    b. electrolysis
    c. photo-epilation
    d. laser hair removal

27. A person who specializes in electrolysis is called a(n):
    a. esthetician
    b. biochemist
    c. electrologist
    d. cosmetologist

28. A necessity for preventing irreparable damage while performing any type of electrolysis is:
    a. client relaxation
    b. proper training
    c. several years of experience
    d. the newest and most expensive equipment

29. All of the following are methods of electrolysis EXCEPT:
    a. blend
    b. Galvanic
    c. thermolysis
    d. photo-epilation

30. Which of the following destroys the hair by using 12 to 14 needles to decompose the papilla?
    a. blend method
    b. Galvanic method
    c. thermolysis method
    d. photo-epilation method

31. Galvanic electrolysis is also known as:
    a. short-wave method
    b. pulsed light method
    c. high frequency method
    d. the "multiple-needle" process

32. All of the following statements about Galvanic electrolysis are true EXCEPT:
    a. current is on for 30 seconds to 2.5 minutes
    b. a high-level current passes into the needle
    c. it destroys the hair by decomposing the papilla
    d. 12 to 14 needles are inserted into individual follicles at a time

33. Which of the following methods involves inserting a single needle into the hair follicle?
    a. blend method
    b. Galvanic method
    c. thermolysis method
    d. laser hair removal method

34. All of the following statements about thermolysis are true EXCEPT:
    a. client feels only a tiny "flash" of heat
    b. involves inserting a single needle into the follicles
    c. current travels to the papilla for less than a second
    d. the wire used is substantially larger than the electrolysis probe

35. The method which consists of a combination of Galvanic and short-wave current is called:
    a. blend method
    b. pulsed light method
    c. photo-epilation method
    d. laser hair removal method

36. Which of the following methods offers best results to clients with excessive or resistant hair growth?
    a. blend method
    b. pulsed light method
    c. photo-epilation method
    d. laser hair removal method

37. The hair removal treatment using wavelengths of light to penetrate and diminish or destroy hair bulbs is called:
    a. blend method
    b. Galvanic method
    c. thermolysis method
    d. laser hair removal method

38. Laser treatment works best on hair that is in the:
    a. anagen stage
    b. catagen phase
    c. telogen phase
    d. delivery phase

39. All of the following statements about photo-epilation hair removal are true EXCEPT:
    a. a burst of energy destroys hair bulbs
    b. it does not use a constant beam of light
    c. large areas of the body can be treated rapidly
    d. there is an increased risk of burning or scarring

40. Which of the following eliminates wax residue from the skin?
    a. wax remover
    b. soothing lotion
    c. hair growth retardant
    d. antiseptic preparation

41. Which of the following slows the growth of hair after waxing?
    a. wax remover
    b. soothing lotion
    c. hair growth retardant
    d. antiseptic preparation

42. Which of the following is NOT a guideline for safety and sanitation during waxing procedures?
    a. discard anything that cannot be sanitized
    b. perform a patch test prior to performing service
    c. wax eyelids, nipples or inside of the nose or ears
    d. always test the temperature of heated wax on your forearm before application

43. All of the following are contraindictions to waxing EXCEPT:
    a. sunburn
    b. active Herpes
    c. varicose veins
    d. low blood pressure

44. Which of the following is an autoimmune disease in which the body's immune system is impaired or begins to fight itself?
    a. cysts
    b. Lupus
    c. diabetes
    d. active Herpes

45. Which of the following should be the first step taken in a basic waxing procedure?
    a. obtain wax
    b. drape client
    c. wash and sanitize hands
    d. apply antiseptic or pre-wax solution

CHAPTER 12 — Makeup

1. The law of color states that, out of all the colors in the universe, only:
   a. one color is pure
   b. two colors are pure
   c. three colors are pure
   d. secondary colors are pure

2. Which of the following is NOT a primary color?
   a. red
   b. blue
   c. yellow
   d. green

3. Which statement listed below is true?
   a. violet contains equal amounts of red and blue
   b. green contains equal amounts of purple and yellow
   c. violet contains equal proportions of blue and orange
   d. orange contains equal proportions of blue and yellow

4. Mixing a primary color with a neighboring secondary color in equal proportions will produce a:
   a. pure color
   b. tertiary color
   c. triadic color
   d. monochromatic color

5. Colors such as brown or gray are created by mixing:
   a. primary and tertiary colors in equal proportions
   b. tertiary and secondary colors in equal proportions
   c. primary, pure and tertiary colors in unequal and equal proportions
   d. primary, secondary and tertiary colors in unequal and equal proportions

6. The position of a color on the color wheel demonstrates its relationship to the:
   a. cool colors
   b. primary colors
   c. tertiary colors
   d. secondary colors

7. What color scheme is used most often to enhance eye color?
   a. triadic
   b. analog
   c. monochromatic
   d. complementary

8. The lightness or darkness of a color is called its:
   a. hue
   b. tint
   c. value
   d. shade

9. What do the terms warm and cool describe about a color?
   a. hue
   b. tint
   c. tone
   d. shade

10. Warm colors do NOT:
    a. contain blue undertones
    b. describe the tones of colors
    c. contain red or yellow undertones
    d. belong in the orange and red half of the color wheel

11. What term describes using the same color with variations in value and intensity throughout an entire makeup design?
    a. triadic
    b. analog
    c. complementary
    d. monochromatic

12. Which of the following statements regarding triadic color schemes is FALSE?
    a. they are often used for more vibrant effects
    b. they are often used for daytime makeup designs
    c. they are more dramatic than monochromatic or analog color schemes
    d. they use three colors located in a triangular position on the color wheel

13. The ideal or classic facial shape is:
    a. oval
    b. pear
    c. round
    d. square

14. All of the following are true about contouring EXCEPT:
    a. it can appear to reshape the face
    b. it can add illusion of increased dimension to the face
    c. dark colors appear to diminish the appearance of features
    d. lighter colors appear to make features or areas appear smaller

15. The art of arranging light and dark so as to produce three dimensional shapes is:
    a. blending
    b. chiaroscuro
    c. makeup essentials
    d. corrective makeup

16. In order to add dimension to an oblong face, a hint of contour should be added directly:
    a. below the cheekbone
    b. above the jawline and eye area
    c. above the cheekbone and blended down the face
    d. below the forehead and blending toward the eye area

17. Which facial shape has a narrow forehead and a wide jawline?
    a. oval
    b. oblong
    c. pear-shaped
    d. heart-shaped

18. What is the result of creating thin, sculpted arches when doing eyebrow design?
    a. dramatic effect
    b. expressionless face
    c. balance and symmetry
    d. narrow forehead and surprised look

19. Which type of eyes require very little contouring, as they are recessed?
    a. bulging
    b. deep-set
    c. drooping
    d. close-set

20. What makeup application does NOT benefit bulging eyes?
    a. blend shadows in horizontal fashion
    b. contour and shade in the protruding lid area
    c. brighter colors and soft shading of the upper and lower lids
    d. "grade" the shadow from dark at the lids to light as you approach the browbone

21. Drawing a line beyond the natural fullness of the lip using lip liner creates a fuller appearance for:
    a. thin lips
    b. uneven lips
    c. full bottom lips
    d. downturned lips

22. The ideal lighting for makeup applications is:
    a. fluorescent only
    b. fluorescent and ultraviolet
    c. incandescent and ultraviolet
    d. fluorescent and incandescent

23. When applying makeup, the facial chair should not recline more than:
    a. 15°
    b. 25°
    c. 35°
    d. 45°

24. All of the following statements describe a benefit derived from using foundation EXCEPT:
    a. heals broken blood vessels
    b. corrects undesirable skin tones
    c. conceals imperfections in the skin
    d. helps protect skin from UV-related damage

25. The most common form of foundation generally preferred because of its sheer, natural coverage and easy application and blending is called:
    a. crème
    b. liquid
    c. powder
    d. pancake

26. Important factors to consider when selecting a foundation include all of the following EXCEPT:
    a. skin type
    b. hair type
    c. time of year
    d. type of finish required

27. Unless correction is required, the general guideline is to match foundation to the:
    a. clothing
    b. eye color
    c. skin tone
    d. hair color

28. A golden skin tone has a:
    a. yellow cast
    b. yellowish-green color
    c. carmel-colored light to dark brown
    d. light, yellow to slightly peach undertone

29. Which of the following foundations should be used for a blue/violet undertone?
    a. yellow
    b. light peach
    c. light brown
    d. medium peach

30. Under-eye circles, broken capillaries, blemishes and dark, shadowed areas of the face can be corrected with:
    a. concealer
    b. foundation
    c. eye shadow
    d. eyebrow color

31. "Wide-set" eyes have a space between the eyes greater than the:
    a. width of an eyebrow
    b. width of an eye
    c. width of two eyes
    d. width of three eyes

32. The area between the base of the lashes and the crease line makes up how much of the eye?
    a. 1/3
    b. 2/3
    c. 4/5
    d. 3/4

33. Liquid and powder eyeliners are usually applied with a:
    a. pen
    b. brush
    c. pencil
    d. marker

34. Which of the following terms is NOT a benefit derived from using mascara?
    a. hides
    b. defines
    c. thickens
    d. lengthens

35. The lip color should not overpower the amount of color applied to the:
    a. nose and eyes
    b. eyelids and eyes
    c. cheeks and eyes
    d. eyebrows and eyes

36. The most common type of lip color is called:
    a. blush
    b. lip liner
    c. lip gloss
    d. lipstick

37. What product purifies and balances the skin's pH levels?
    a. toner
    b. exfoliator
    c. eye crème
    d. moisturizer

38. What product removes excess surface skin cells?
    a. blush
    b. concealer
    c. exfoliator
    d. foundation

39. A makeup product that accentuates and defines the shape of the eyes is:
    a. eyeliner
    b. mascara
    c. eye shadow
    d. eyebrow pencil/powder

40. The purpose of lip liner is to:
    a. add color to the lips
    b. add high shine to the lips
    c. add texture and fullness to the lips
    d. defines or corrects the shape of the lips

41. What makeup implement is used to remove product from a container?
    a. brush
    b. spatula
    c. tweezer
    d. latex sponges

42. Tweezers are used for all of the following EXCEPT:
    a. curling lashes
    b. shaping eyebrows
    c. removing stray hairs
    d. applying artificial lashes

43. A makeup application is:
    a. 20% art and 80% science
    b. 80% art and 20% science
    c. 40% art and 60% science
    d. 60% art and 40% science

44. Which of the conditions below would most likely NOT be a prospective client for camouflage makeup?
    a. victim of a fire
    b. cancer survivor
    c. client with a sunburn
    d. client with a congenital disfigurement

45. Approximately how long does it take to perform an eyelash or eyebrow tinting procedure?
    a. 10 minutes
    b. 20 minutes
    c. 30 minutes
    d. 40 minutes

CHAPTER 13 — Advanced Treatments

1. All of the following are contraindications for performing an advanced treatment EXCEPT:
   a. sunburn
   b. fungal infections
   c. emotional distress
   d. high blood pressure

2. Which of the following hand and foot treatment products are used to hydrate, calm and soothe the skin?
   a. mask
   b. exfoliant
   c. sugar scrub
   d. massage lubricant

3. Which of the following hand and foot treatment products soften skin by removing dead skin cells?
   a. mask
   b. exfoliant
   c. essential oil
   d. massage lubricant

4. The exfoliating treatment in which a layer of crème is applied to the skin, allowed to dry and then rubbed away is called:
   a. gomage
   b. manual exfoliant
   c. hand-held exfoliant
   d. synthetic microbead

5. What two principles give wraps the ability to create temporary tightness?
   a. absorption and secretion
   b. circulation and absorption
   c. compaction and circulation
   d. absorption and compaction

6. Prior to a body wrap, the bandages may be soaked in:
   a. cleanser
   b. body lotion
   c. antibacterial wash
   d. aromatherapy toning solution

7. Which of the following cellulite wrap products is used to wrap the body and increase product penetration and treatment results?
   a. cellulite gel
   b. cellophane
   c. cellulite crème
   d. skin purifying wipes

8. The method of water therapy in which the client is sprayed with water, seawater or mineral water infused with herbs or essential oils is called:
   a. steam baths
   b. balneotherapy
   c. affusion therapy
   d. hydrotherapy tub treatment

9. Superficial or light chemical peels affect:
   a. only the dermis
   b. only the epidermis
   c. all layers of the skin
   d. the dermis and epidermis

10. Which of the following treatments offers a light resurfacing of the epidermis?
    a. reflexology
    b. dermabrasion
    c. microdermabrasion
    d. aluminum oxide crystals

11. The degree of exfoliation during microdermabrasion depends on all of the following EXCEPT:
    a. level of crystal spray
    b. time of day performed
    c. number of passes over the skin
    d. number of treatments performed

12. How many microdermabrasion treatments are required to achieve noticeable improvement?
    a. 1 to 2
    b. 5 to 10
    c. 6 to 12
    d. 15 to 20

13. Which of the following treatments requires a patient to be anesthetized?
    a. reflexology
    b. dermabrasion
    c. microdermabrasion
    d. aluminum oxide crystals

14. If the client's skin is noticeably pink after the first pass of the microdermabrasion machine over the face, the esthetician should:
    a. call a physician
    b. perform additional passes
    c. not perform a second pass
    d. soak the client's skin with cool water

15. For what length of time should the esthetician advise the client to avoid saunas and steam following a microdermabrasion treatment?
    a. 6 to 8 hours
    b. 10 to 15 hours
    c. 24 to 48 hours
    d. 60 to 72 hours

16. Which of the following is a technique that uses finger-point pressure to influence certain body conditions?
    a. reflexology
    b. dermabrasion
    c. cellulite treatments
    d. manual lymphatic drainage massage

17. Which of the following fluids is responsible for delivering nutrients to cells and carrying away cellular waste before it becomes toxic to the body?
    a. MLD
    b. water
    c. lymph
    d. alcohol

18. Which of the following treatments uses a gentle pumping technique to help eliminate toxins, waste and excess water from the face and body?
    a. reflexology
    b. dermabrasion
    c. cellulite massage treatments
    d. manual lymphatic drainage massage (MLD)

19. The treatment that increases circulation, promoting the removal of excess fluids and waste material as well as firming the muscle tissue is known as:
    a. reflexology
    b. microdermabrasion
    c. cellulite massage treatments
    d. manual lymphatic drainage massage (MLD)

20. Which of the following refers to the medicinal use of plants?
    a. algotherapy
    b. phytotherapy
    c. aromatherapy
    d. phytocosmetics

21. Chemicals such as alkaloids and glucosides that give plants their healing properties are called:
    a. tinctures
    b. antimicrobials
    c. active ingredients
    d. inactive ingredients

22. Which of the following natural substances relieves pain either by relaxing muscles or reducing pain signals to the brain?
    a. analgesic
    b. antioxidant
    c. antibacterial
    d. antimicrobial

23. The natural substance that is responsible for killing a wide range of harmful bacteria, fungi and viruses is called a(n):
    a. astringent
    b. antioxidant
    c. antimicrobial
    d. circulatory stimulant

24. The natural substance that prevents bacterial growth on the skin with external application is called a(n):
    a. emollient
    b. antiseptic
    c. astringent
    d. rubefacient

25. Which of the following provides a constricting, drying effect and helps contract tissue and reduce secretions?
    a. emollient
    b. antiseptic
    c. astringent
    d. rubefacient

26. The natural substance that increases blood flow at the surface of the skin is called a(n):
    a. nervine
    b. relaxant
    c. emollient
    d. circulatory stimulant

27. Which of the following natural substances softens, soothes and protects the skin?
    a. emollient
    b. astringent
    c. rubefacient
    d. circulatory stimulant

28. Commercial extractions that require soaking an herb in alcohol to extract the active ingredient from the plant are known as:
    a. tinctures
    b. ointments
    c. glucosides
    d. active ingredients

29. A thick crème or salve made from the combination of herbs and petroleum is called a(n):
    a. tincture
    b. ointment
    c. glucoside
    d. active ingredient

30. Which of the following is created by steeping an herb in boiling water?
    a. poultice
    b. infusion
    c. decoction
    d. fomentation

31. Soaking a clean towel in the liquid from both an infusion and decoction and applying it to a specific area of the body is known as:
    a. poultice
    b. Ayurveda
    c. fomentation
    d. aromatherapy

32. Which of the following is the controlled use of essential oils?
    a. algotherapy
    b. fomentation
    c. phytotherapy
    d. aromatherapy

33. The category of fragrance that is the easiest to identify is:
    a. floral
    b. oriental
    c. spice blend
    d. floral bouquet

34. Which of the following is the largest category of fragrance?
    a. floral
    b. oriental
    c. spice blend
    d. floral bouquet

35. All of the following are scents in the fruit blend category EXCEPT:
    a. apple
    b. melon
    c. almond
    d. pomegranate

36. Which of the following categories of fragrance represents concoctions from several different scents?
    a. fruit blend
    b. forest blend
    c. floral bouquet
    d. modern blend

37. Which of the following categories of oils helps to destroy bacteria and heal skin eruptions?
    a. healing oils
    b. analgesic oils
    c. antiseptic oils
    d. astringent oils

38. Which of the following types of oils reduce inflammation and soothe swollen muscles?
    a. healing oils
    b. analgesic oils
    c. antioxidant oils
    d. anti-inflammatory oils

39. Oils that promote cells to regenerate so the skin can repair itself are called:
    a. healing oils
    b. soothing oils
    c. moisturizing oils
    d. anti-inflammatory oils

40. Which of the following types of oils are responsible for softening dry or flaky skin?
    a. healing oils
    b. soothing oils
    c. stimulating oils
    d. moisturizing oils

41. Which of the following is the most common method for obtaining essential oils?
    a. extraction
    b. enfleurage
    c. expression
    d. steam distillation

42. A common method for obtaining essential oils that involves squeezing out an ingredient's fragrant oil is known as:
    a. extraction
    b. enfleurage
    c. expression
    d. maceration

43. Which of the following methods for obtaining essential oils uses a chemical solvent to leach the aromatic component from an ingredient?
    a. expression
    b. maceration
    c. steam distillation
    d. commercial extraction

44. The essential oil that is often used in treating acne is called:
   a. rose
   b. tea tree
   c. lavender
   b. ylang-ylang

45. Which of the following essential oils can be used in therapies aimed at treating sore muscles?
   a. neroli
   b. tea tree
   c. chamomile
   d. sandalwood

CHAPTER 14 — Estheticians in the Medical Field

1. A physician who specializes in diagnosing and treating diseases of the skin and nails is known as a(n):
   a. dentist
   b. obstetrician
   c. medical doctor
   d. dermatologist

2. All of the following are properties of desquamation of the stratum corneum EXCEPT:
   a. peeling
   b. shedding
   c. coming off in scales
   d. reduction of pore size

3. Which type of peel can be performed by an esthetician in a skin care center?
   a. deep peel
   b. light peel
   c. phenol peel
   d. medium-depth peel

4. The agency that has established procedural guidelines to ensure safety and consistency in the use of alpha hydroxy acids (AHAs) for chemical peels is referred to as:
   a. CSI
   b. FDA
   c. OSHA
   d. EMDA

5. Regardless of the type of peel performed, direct sun exposure must be avoided for:
   a. one week
   b. two weeks
   c. one month
   d. two or three months

6. Chemical peels are recommended for which of the following descriptive statements?
   a. dry, dark-colored skin
   b. dry, light-colored skin
   c. moist, light-colored skin
   d. fair skin with superficial wrinkles

7. Deep peels are recommended for treating deep facial wrinkles, sun-damaged skin and:
   a. fine wrinkles
   b. surface wrinkles
   c. superficial blemishes
   d. uneven pigmentation

8. Which of the following treatments fill in creased, furrowed or sunken facial skin, lines and wrinkles?
   a. deep peel
   b. dermabrasion
   c. Botox® injections
   d. collagen or fat injection

9. Collagen or fat injections usually last for how many months?
   a. 1-2 months
   b. 3-6 months
   c. 8-9 months
   d. 10-12 months

10. Which of the following is NOT a result of collagen or fat injections?
    a. addition of fullness to lips
    b. plumping up of facial skin
    c. evening out of pigmentation
    d. decreasing of indentations in the skin

11. Which of the following procedures is used to treat sunken cheeks, laugh lines, skin depressions or indentations, forehead wrinkles or to enlarge lips?
    a. fat injection
    b. chemical peel
    c. Botox injection
    d. cosmetic surgery

12. What surgical procedure improves uneven skin textures by mechanically scraping off the top layers of the skin?
    a. fat injection
    b. dermabrasion
    c. Botox injection
    d. collagen injection

13. Dermabrasion is used to treat all of the following EXCEPT:
    a. acne scars
    b. pigmentation
    c. deep wrinkles
    d. sunken cheeks

14. Which of the following, known as eyelid surgery, is used to remove excess fat, skin or muscle from the upper and lower eyelids?
    a. rhinoplasty
    b. rhytidectomy
    c. blepharoplasty
    d. laser resurfacing

15. All of the following are side-effects of blepharoplasty EXCEPT:
    a. tightness of lids
    b. excessive tearing
    c. reduction of jowls
    d. temporary blurred vision

16. Which type of cosmetic surgery is recommended for patients with drooping upper eyelids or puffy bags below the eyes?
    a. rhytidectomy
    b. chemical peel
    c. blepharoplasty
    d. laser resurfacing

17. Which of the following can improve visible signs of aging by removing excess fat, tightening underlying muscles and re-draping the skin of the face and neck?
    a. rhinoplasty
    b. rhytidectomy
    c. blepharoplasty
    d. laser resurfacing

18. Which type of cosmetic surgery is recommended for individuals whose face and neck have begun to sag but still have some elasticity in their facial skin and good bone structure?
    a. rhytidectomy
    b. chemical peel
    c. blepharoplasty
    d. laser resurfacing

19. Results of rhytidectomy include all of the following EXCEPT:
    a. reduction of jowls
    b. making loose neck skin more taut
    c. improvement of sagging facial skin
    d. improvement of irregularities from acne scars and wrinkles

20. Which type of cosmetic surgery uses a beam of highly focused light to vaporize the upper layers of damaged skin at specific and controlled levels of penetration?
    a. rhytidectomy
    b. dermabrasion
    c. blepharoplasty
    d. laser resurfacing

21. Which type of laser removes the affected portion of the epidermis to heat the papillary dermis to regenerate collagen?
    a. ablative
    b. non-ablative
    c. carbon monoxide
    d. short pulsed erbium

22. Laser resurfacing is recommended for patients seeking treatment for:
    a. fine lines
    b. deep acne scars
    c. drooping upper eyelids
    d. sagging face and neck skin

23. Following a laser resurfacing treatment, how long should a patient wait before normal activities can be resumed?
    a. 1 week
    b. 2 weeks
    c. 3 weeks
    d. 4 weeks

24. Which type of post-operative complication develops when microbes invade an inured, open or wounded part of the body?
    a. conjunctivitis
    b. yeast infection
    c. herpetic infection
    d. bacterial infection

25. What is a superficial infection called that occurs on moist areas of the skin?
    a. conjunctivitis
    b. yeast infection
    c. herpetic infection
    d. bacterial infection

26. A highly contagious viral infection that is triggered when the body or skin is placed under extreme stress, such as a laser treatment, is known as:
    a. ecchymosis
    b. conjunctivitis
    c. yeast infection
    d. herpetic infection

27. Which post-operative complication has undesirable side-effects such as having red, itchy and watery eyes that may develop a significant amount of pus?
    a. ecchymosis
    b. conjunctivitis
    c. yeast infection
    d. herpetic infection

28. What post-operative complication includes extreme symptoms of redness and clusters or large patches of pustules which can later develop into scaly patches?
    a. conjunctivitis
    b. yeast infection
    c. herpetic infection
    d. bacterial infection

29. The clinical term for bruising of the skin is:
    a. scarring
    b. erythema
    c. ecchymosis
    d. conjunctivitis

30. What is the clinical term for redness?
    a. scarring
    b. erythema
    c. ecchymosis
    d. conjunctivitis

31. Which of the following degree of burns is the least severe and only damages the epidermis?
   a. first-degree
   b. second-degree
   c. third-degree
   d. fourth-degree

32. Damage from which type of burn penetrates to the dermis, resulting in redness, swelling and blistering?
   a. first-degree burn
   b. second-degree burn
   c. third-degree burn
   d. fourth-degree burn

33. To care for a second-degree burn, the burned area should be:
   a. treated with aloe vera
   b. treated with an ointment
   c. immersed in cool water
   d. covered tightly with sterile gauze

34. The most severe burn which damages or destroys underlying tissue, exposes nerve endings, and burns fat, muscle and bone is known as a:
   a. first-degree burn
   b. second-degree burn
   c. third-degree burn
   d. fourth-degree burn

35. Taking a section of healthy skin from an unburned area of the body and surgically reattaching it to cover the burned area is called:
   a. rhinoplasty
   b. ecchymosis
   c. rhytidectomy
   d. skin grafting

36. Third-degree burns are frequently treated with a(n):
    a. aloe vera
    b. Isotretinoin
    c. topical medication
    d. antimicrobial dressing

37. Which of the following is NOT an example of a topical medication?
    a. antihistamines
    b. keratolytic medications
    c. antibacterial medications
    d. anti-inflammatory medications

38. Which of the following is a topical medication used to treat inflammatory conditions such as dermatitis?
    a. antibiotics
    b. antihistamines
    c. keratolytic medications
    d. anti-inflammatory medications

39. Crèmes or ointments used to promote rapid cell turnover and exfoliation are referred to as:
    a. antibiotics
    b. antihistamines
    c. keratolytic medications
    d. antibacterial medications

40. Which type of medication is used to kill bacteria and prevent them from reproducing?
    a. antihistamine
    b. keratolytic medication
    c. antibacterial medication
    d. anti-inflammatory medication

41. What is the name given to medications that are taken orally and travel through the body in the bloodstream?
    a. topical
    b. systemic
    c. keratolytic
    d. antibacterial

42. Which type of systemic medication is used to kill or prevent the growth of bacteria?
    a. Accutane
    b. antibiotic
    c. keratolytic
    d. antihistamine

43. The medication that is frequently prescribed to relieve uncomfortable skin conditions such as itching and hives is a(n):
    a. Accutane
    b. antibiotic
    c. keratolytic
    d. antihistamine

44. Which of the following treatments would most likely require an esthetician to seek additional training and/or work under a physician's supervision?
    a. leg waxing
    b. basic facial
    c. light chemical peel
    d. TCA chemical peel

45. The procedures that may be legally performed, as defined by a local regulatory agency are referred to as the:
    a. medical code
    b. scope of practice
    c. educational practice
    d. continuing education law

FINAL EXAM

1. The average number of hours of sleep needed per night to function properly is:
   a. two to three hours
   b. four to five hours
   c. six to eight hours
   d. nine to eleven hours

2. Stress can be managed effectively by:
   a. avoiding stress at all costs
   b. maintaining moderation and balance
   c. giving full attention to all stressful situations
   d. becoming aggressive, assertive or outspoken

3. What does RDA refer to?
   a. Required Dairy Allotment
   b. Requested Dental Appointment
   c. Required Diet Association
   d. Recommended Dietary Allowances

4. What energy-producing substances are contained in almost all foods?
   a. nutrition, exercise and rest
   b. calories, proteins and water
   c. minerals, proteins and calories
   d. carbohydrates, proteins and fats

5. Handling clients with tact is:
   a. offensive to the client
   b. detrimental to the client's confidence in the esthetician
   c. not important in building professional relationships
   d. very important in building professional relationships

6. A necessary companion piece to the resumé that introduces you to the prospective employer is a:
   a. cover letter
   b. job interview
   c. business card
   d. performance review

7. Developing relationships with individuals who can make contact with potential customers or employers is called:
   a. retailing
   b. networking
   c. communication
   d. correspondence

8. The most effective form of advertising is:
   a. direct mail
   b. newspaper ads
   c. word-of-mouth
   d. web page banners

9. The size of a product's container, the aroma or a specific ingredient of the product are its:
   a. benefits
   b. features
   c. promotions
   d. market trends

10. What a product will do to enhance the appearance or improve the condition of the client's skin are the product's:
    a. features
    b. benefits
    c. promotions
    d. common goals

11. A business owned by one person who is in complete control is called a:
    a. franchise
    b. corporation
    c. partnership
    d. sole proprietorship

12. An advisor on borrowing money, signing rental agreements and assuming tax responsibilities is a(n):
    a. lawyer
    b. distributor
    c. stockholder
    d. insurance agent

13. The reservoir of cash that is needed to stay ahead of creditors is called:
    a. net worth
    b. total liabilities
    c. operating capital
    d. improvement costs

14. Which of the following insurance policies is required by law?
    a. premise
    b. property
    c. malpractice
    d. worker's compensation

15. A skin care center should keep all records of daily sales and services for at least:
    a. one week
    b. six months
    c. nine months
    d. one year

16. Which of the following describes how you plan to attract attention to your skin care center and create a positive impression?
    a. advertising
    b. business plan
    c. product knowledge
    d. inventory and product control

17. One-celled microorganisms that are either disease-producing or nondisease producing are called:
    a. virus
    b. bacteria
    c. parasites
    d. immunity

18. Head lice, itch mites, ringworm and nail fungus are all diseases caused by:
    a. infection
    b. internal parasites
    c. external parasites
    d. bloodborne pathogens

19. A contagious disease refers to a disease that is:
    a. vaccinated
    b. immunized
    c. not spread from one person to another
    d. easily spread from one person to another

20. All of the following could indicate an allergic reaction to latex EXCEPT:
    a. hives
    b. itching
    c. swelling
    d. virus

21. The second level of infection control that does not eliminate bacterial spores is called:
    a. efficacy
    b. sanitation
    c. disinfection
    d. contamination

22. All of the following porous products used in the skin care center can be properly disinfected EXCEPT:
    a. lancets and tweezers
    b. probes and extractors
    c. tweezers and extractors
    d. sponges and disposable files

23. Tools and instruments used to puncture or invade the skin must be sterilized or:
    a. sanitized
    b. disinfected
    c. immunized
    d. disposable

24. How do you react in the event of a cut, scratch or embedded object eye injury?
    a. try to remove embedded object
    b. flush with warm water
    c. apply pressure to the wound
    d. secure gauze pad or cloth with a bandage

25. The study of the organs and systems of the body is called:
    a. anatomy
    b. osteology
    c. physiology
    d. ergonomics

26. Which of the following is the control center of cell activities?
    a. nucleus
    b. cytoplasm
    c. protoplasm
    d. cell membrane

27. Groups of cells of the same kind make up:
    a. bones
    b. organs
    c. glands
    d. tissues

28. Separate body structures that perform specific functions are:
    a. cells
    b. organs
    c. tissues
    d. systems

29. Which of the following is NOT a type of muscle tissue?
    a. cardiac
    b. myology
    c. voluntary
    d. involuntary

30. Blood is transported through all of the following vessels EXCEPT:
    a. veins
    b. arteries
    c. capillaries
    d. maxillaries

31. The body's state of balance is referred to as:
    a. osteology
    b. anabolism
    c. homeostasis
    d. metabolism

32. The lower respiratory tract consists of all of the following EXCEPT:
    a. lungs
    b. larynx
    c. trachea
    d. bronchi

33. Light, heat, chemical and magnetic changes are all produced by:
    a. force
    b. electricity
    c. insulators
    d. short circuit

34. Which of the following is NOT a unit of measurement for electricity?
    a. amp
    b. volt
    c. watt
    d. conductor

35. More current flowing through a line than the line is designed to carry is called a(n):
    a. cathode
    b. overload
    c. spark gap
    d. power box

36. All of the following are protocols of fire prevention EXCEPT:
    a. install lighted exit signs
    b. inspect fire safety devices
    c. use frayed and exposed wires
    d. store flammable materials properly

37. Having opposite poles in an electrical current is referred to as:
    a. polarity
    b. radiation
    c. electrode
    d. Galvanic Current

38. All of the following statements are benefits of Direct High Frequency EXCEPT:
    a. stimulates surface tissue
    b. stimulates sebum production
    c. heals existing papules and pustules
    d. increases circulation and blood flow

39. Infrared rays can penetrate all layers of the skin and have the ability to affect all of the following EXCEPT:
    a. blood
    b. bones
    c. nerves
    d. muscles

40. The most commonly used machine that is a combination of different electrical units into one piece of equipment is called a(n):
    a. atomizer
    b. paraffin unit
    c. multifunction machine
    d. microdermabrasion machine

41. Anything that occupies space is called:
    a. matter
    b. energy
    c. chemistry
    d. combustion

42. All of the following statements are true about liquids EXCEPT:
    a. they have definite shape
    b. they have definite weight
    c. they have definite volume
    d. they take the shape of the container in which they are poured

43. Which of the following is the most abundant element in the earth's crust?
    a. carbon
    b. oxygen
    c. nitrogen
    d. hydrogen

44. The branch of science that deals with the chemicals related to life processes and their reactions within the body is called:
    a. anatomy
    b. biochemistry
    c. organic chemistry
    d. inorganic chemistry

45. All of the following statements about carbohydrates are true EXCEPT:
    a. they play a key role in metabolism
    b. they are used by the body to store energy
    c. they are used to construct and renew the body
    d. glucose is the most important carbohydrate for providing energy

46. All of the following statements regarding aerosols are true EXCEPT:
    a. they are explosive and flammable
    b. they are products packaged under pressure
    c. they are environmentally friendly to discard
    d. they are blended with a propellant inside a container

47. Ingredients responsible for producing the desired effect are called:
    a. surfactants
    b. humectants
    c. active ingredients
    d. inactive ingredients

48. Which of the following are organic ingredients that bind water and deposit it onto the skin?
    a. fatty acids
    b. emollients
    c. surfactants
    d. humectants

49. Acids or bases used to adjust the desired product pH level are called:
    a. comedogenic
    b. pH adjustors
    c. active ingredients
    d. non-comedogenic

50. All of the following statements about lighteners are true EXCEPT:
    a. they are used at relatively high levels
    b. they slowly block the production of melanin in the skin
    c. they are used to bleach or lighten areas of hyperpigmentation
    d. they usually take months of continued use to deliver a noticeable effect

51. All of the following are functions of the skin EXCEPT:
    a. secretion
    b. protection
    c. absorption
    d. excoriation

52. Which of the following is NOT one of the main layers of the skin?
    a. dermal
    b. tendon
    c. epidermal
    d. subcutaneous

53. A strong protein substance that, when broken down, forms bundles that strengthen and give structure to the skin is:
    a. scars
    b. dermis
    c. keloids
    d. collagen

54. Apocrine glands are located on all of the following parts of the body EXCEPT the:
    a. feet
    b. nipples
    c. genitals
    d. underarm area

55. What is the name of the connective tissue that holds bones to other bones to form joints?
    a. tendons
    b. muscles
    c. cartilage
    d. ligaments

56. All of the following are factors of skin absorption EXCEPT:
    a. hair follicles
    b. hydration level
    c. oiliness of the skin
    d. temperature of the skin

57. Acne can be caused by all of the following EXCEPT:
    a. genetics
    b. emotional stress
    c. hormonal changes
    d. eating too much chocolate

58. The congenital disease that results in the failure of the skin to produce melanin is called:
    a. vitiligo
    b. albinism
    c. leukoderma
    d. hyperpigmentation

59. Which of the following is the number one factor in extrinsic aging?
    a. diabetes
    b. smoking
    c. physical effects of aging
    d. amount of sun exposure

60. The general appearance of sun-damaged skin shows all of the following major structural changes EXCEPT:
    a. a leathery face
    b. irregular pigment
    c. a significant increase of elasticity
    d. numerous fine lines and wrinkles

61. All of the following are ways to greet a client professionally and respectfully EXCEPT:
    a. offer a friendly smile
    b. avoid direct eye contact
    c. welcome the client warmly
    d. extend your hand and shake hands firmly

62. A lifestyle factor that robs nutrients and oxygen from the skin is:
    a. diet
    b. exercise
    c. smoking
    d. proper nutritition

63. The size of the pores is most visible on the:
    a. eye area
    b. chin area
    c. cheek area
    d. forehead area

64. The results that the ingredients deliver are called:
    a. labels
    b. features
    c. benefits
    d. product statement

65. Which of the following is NOT a purpose of a care call?
    a. skin reaction
    b. client satisfaction
    c. product effectiveness
    d. the purchase of products for home care

66. All of the following are elements of proper skin care that combine to result in healthy, glowing skin EXCEPT:
    a. regular exercise
    b. a well-balanced diet
    c. an adequate intake of water
    d. excessive exposure to the sun

67. The most effective sunscreens contain ingredients that act as:
    a. blockers
    b. absorbers
    c. both blockers and absorbers
    d. neither blockers nor absorbers

68. A systematic, therapeutic method of manipulating the body by rubbing, pinching, tapping, kneading or stroking is known as:
    a. massage
    b. hydration
    c. dehydration
    d. contraindication

69. Which of the following areas should NOT be stimulated by petrissage movements?
    a. eyes
    b. arms
    c. shoulders
    d. upper back

70. Which of the following skin types displays few breakouts or clogged areas?
    a. dry
    b. oily
    c. normal
    d. combination

Salon Fundamentals™ *Esthetics*

71. Which of the following is a vascular disorder characterized by flushed redness, dilated capillaries and small red bumps?
    a. acne
    b. rosacea
    c. couperose
    d. dehydration

72. The skin care product that assists in cleansing the skin and returning normal to dry skin to a normal pH is a(n):
    a. antiseptic
    b. astringent
    c. manual exfoliant
    d. chemical exfoliant

73. A highly alkaline solution that liquefies sebum is known as:
    a. toner
    b. Galvanic current
    c. massage crème
    d. desincrustation solution

74. Excessive hair growth which is genetically determined is called:
    a. capilli
    b. hirsutism
    c. supercilia
    d. hypertrichosis

75. Thick, coarse hair that grows on the face to form a beard is called:
    a. cilia
    b. capilli
    c. barba
    d. lanugo

76. All of the following are phases of the hair life cycle EXCEPT:
    a. telogen phase
    b. anagen phase
    c. catagen phase
    d. lanugo phase

77. The most popular waxing service in the skin care center is the:
    a. chin
    b. back
    c. upper lip
    d. bikini line

78. The majority of professional waxing services are performed with:
    a. soft wax
    b. hard wax
    c. sugar paste
    d. low-level current

79. Which method is a combination of Galvanic and short-wave current:
    a. blend method
    b. pulsed light method
    c. photo-epilation method
    d. laser hair removal method

80. All of the following statements about photo-epilation hair removal are true EXCEPT:
    a. a burst of energy destroys hair bulbs
    b. it does not use a constant beam of light
    c. large areas of the body can be treated rapidly
    d. there is an increased risk of burning or scarring

81. All of the following are contraindictions to waxing EXCEPT:
    a. sunburn
    b. active Herpes
    c. varicose veins
    d. low blood pressure

82. All of the following are primary colors EXCEPT:
    a. red
    b. blue
    c. yellow
    d. green

83. The color scheme used most often to enhance eye color is called:
    a. triadic
    b. analog
    c. monochromatic
    d. complementary

84. The ideal or classic facial shape is:
    a. oval
    b. pear
    c. round
    d. square

85. All of the following statements describe a benefit derived from using foundation EXCEPT:
    a. heals broken blood vessels
    b. corrects undesirable skin tones
    c. conceals imperfections in the skin
    d. help protects skin for UV-related damage

86. "Wide-set" eyes have a space between the eyes greater than the:
    a. width of an eyebrow
    b. width of an eye
    c. width of two eyes
    d. width of three eyes

87. A product that purifies and balances the skin's pH levels is a(n):
    a. toner
    b. exfoliator
    c. eye crème
    d. moisturizer

88. A makeup application is:
    a. 20% art and 80% science
    b. 80% art and 20% science
    c. 40% art and 60% science
    d. 60% art and 40% science

89. How does an exfoliant soften skin?
    a. disinfects the skin
    b. moisturizes the skin
    c. removes hair from the surface of the skin
    d. removes dead skin cells from the surface of the skin

90. The treatment which requires a patient to be anesthetized is called:
    a. reflexology
    b. dermabrasion
    c. microdermabrasion
    d. aluminum oxide crystals

91. The natural substance that prevents bacterial growth on the skin with external application is called a(n):
    a. emollient
    b. antiseptic
    c. astringent
    d. rubefacient

92. Soaking a clean towel in the liquid from both an infusion and decoction and applying it to a specific area of the body is known as:
    a. poultice
    b. Ayurveda
    c. fomentation
    d. aromatherapy

93. All of the following are scents in the fruit blend category EXCEPT:
    a. apple
    b. melon
    c. almond
    d. pomegranate

94. The therapeutic use of marine plants to cleanse and revitalize the skin and body is known as:
    a. algotherapy
    b. phytotherapy
    c. aromatherapy
    d. microdermabrasion

95. A physician who specializes in diagnosing and treating diseases of the skin and nails is known as a(n):
    a. dentist
    b. obstetrician
    c. medical doctor
    d. dermatologist

96. Which of the following is NOT a result of collagen or fat injections?
    a. addition of fullness to lips
    b. plumping up of facial skin
    c. evening out of pigmentation
    d. decreasing of indentations in the skin

97. Dermabrasion is used to treat all of the following EXCEPT:
    a. acne scars
    b. pigmentation
    c. deep wrinkles
    d. sunken cheeks

98. Why is a superficial fungal infection able to occur on specific areas of the skin?
    a. the skin remains dry
    b. the skin remains moist
    c. bacteria invades wrinkled skin
    d. dehydrated skin produces yeast

99. What is the clinical term for redness?
    a. scarring
    b. erythema
    c. ecchymosis
    d. conjunctivitis

100. The procedures that may be legally performed, as defined by a local regulatory agency are referred to as the:
    a. medical code
    b. scope of practice
    c. educational practice
    d. continuing education law

Answer Key: CHAPTER 1 — Personal Development

1.	c –	3	13.	c –	8	25.	c –	16
2.	d –	3	14.	a –	8	26.	c –	17
3.	d –	4	15.	a –	8	27.	d –	18
4.	b –	5	16.	b –	9	28.	a –	19
5.	b –	5	17.	d –	10	29.	b –	19
6.	d –	5	18.	b –	10	30.	d –	19
7.	b –	5	19.	d –	11	31.	b –	20
8.	d –	5	20.	d –	11	32.	c –	21
9.	d –	5	21.	b –	12	33.	c –	21
10.	d –	7	22.	d –	12	34.	a –	22
11.	a –	7	23.	d –	13	35.	a –	23
12.	a –	7	24.	d –	15			

Answer Key: CHAPTER 2 — Professional Development

1.	b –	33	8.	b –	44	15.	b –	52
2.	d –	35	9.	c –	45	16.	b –	54
3.	c –	35	10.	c –	48	17.	b –	56
4.	a –	35	11.	d –	49	18.	a –	57
5.	d –	38	12.	a –	50	19.	b –	61
6.	c –	41	13.	d –	50	20.	d –	64
7.	d –	42	14.	b –	52			

Answer Key: CHAPTER 3 — Business Basics

1.	b – 70	11.	b – 75	21.	d – 80
2.	b – 71	12.	d – 75	22.	a – 81
3.	d – 71	13.	d – 76	23.	d – 81
4.	c – 71	14.	c – 77	24.	c – 81
5.	d – 72	15.	b – 78	25.	b – 81
6.	c – 72	16.	a – 79	26.	b – 82
7.	c – 72	17.	c – 79	27.	d – 84
8.	c – 73	18.	d – 79	28.	d – 84
9.	a – 74	19.	c – 80	29.	b – 84
10.	c – 74	20.	a – 80	30.	c – 85

Answer Key: CHAPTER 4 — Skin Care Center Ecology

1.	d – 99	18.	d – 105	35.	d – 113
2.	b – 99	19.	d – 105	36.	b – 113
3.	d – 99	20.	a – 106	37.	d – 115
4.	d – 100	21.	c – 106	38.	b – 116
5.	a – 101	22.	a – 106	39.	d – 116
6.	d – 101	23.	d – 106	40.	a – 116
7.	b – 101	24.	a – 107	41.	d – 117
8.	b – 101	25.	d – 107	42.	d – 118
9.	a – 102	26.	d – 107	43.	c – 118
10.	c – 102	27.	d – 108	44.	c – 120
11.	c – 102	28.	b – 108	45.	b – 120
12.	b – 102	29.	d – 108	46.	c – 122
13.	b – 103	30.	a – 110	47.	d – 124
14.	d – 103	31.	c – 112	48.	b – 125
15.	c – 104	32.	d – 112	49.	a – 126
16.	a – 104	33.	d – 112	50.	a – 126
17.	b – 104	34.	d – 113		

Answer Key: CHAPTER 5— Anatomy

1. a – 131	35. d – 145	69. d – 159
2. a – 132	36. c – 145	70. d – 159
3. a – 132	37. a – 146	71. c – 159
4. a – 132	38. d – 147	72. a – 160
5. b – 132	39. b – 147	73. d – 160
6. a – 133	40. d – 148	74. c – 161
7. c – 133	41. d – 148	75. b – 161
8. d – 133	42. d – 149	76. a – 161
9. c – 133	43. b – 149	77. b – 161
10. d – 134	44. b – 152	78. c – 161
11. a – 134	45. c – 152	79. c – 162
12. c – 134	46. d – 152	80. d – 162
13. c – 134	47. d – 152	81. d – 162
14. b – 134	48. b – 153	82. a – 164
15. d – 135	49. d – 153	83. c – 164
16. c – 135	50. b – 153	84. b – 164
17. a – 136	51. d – 153	85. d – 164
18. a – 136	52. d – 154	86. a – 165
19. b – 136	53. d – 154	87. b – 165
20. c – 136	54. b – 154	88. c – 165
21. a – 137	55. c – 154	89. b – 165
22. d – 137	56. a – 155	90. b – 166
23. c – 138	57. a – 156	91. c – 166
24. d – 138	58. c – 156	92. c – 166
25. d – 139	59. d – 156	93. a – 167
26. a – 142	60. d – 157	94. c – 167
27. c – 142	61. a – 157	95. a – 167
28. a – 143	62. c – 157	96. b – 167
29. b – 143	63. b – 158	97. b – 169
30. b – 143	64. a – 158	98. b – 170
31. d – 143	65. d – 158	99. d – 171
32. b – 144	66. c – 159	100. d – 171
33. c – 144	67. b – 159	
34. b – 144	68. c – 159	

Answer Key: CHAPTER 6 — Electricity and Electrical Equipment

1. b – 176	16. b – 180	31. b – 189
2. c – 176	17. a – 180	32. b – 190
3. d – 176	18. c – 181	33. d – 191
4. d – 176	19. c – 181	34. d – 191
5. a – 176	20. d – 182	35. b – 192
6. d – 177	21. a – 182	36. d – 195
7. a – 177	22. c – 182	37. a – 195
8. d – 177	23. c – 183	38. c – 196
9. c – 177	24. c – 185	39. a – 197
10. a – 178	25. c – 186	40. d – 198
11. a – 178	26. c – 186	41. c – 199
12. d – 178	27. a – 187	42. d – 199
13. c – 179	28. b – 187	43. b – 203
14. a – 180	29. b – 187	44. b – 204
15. b – 180	30. a – 187	45. b – 205

Answer Key: CHAPTER 7 — Chemistry

1. d – 218	18. c – 225	35. b – 238
2. a – 218	19. c – 226	36. c – 239
3. a – 218	20. a – 226	37. a – 239
4. b – 218	21. b – 228	38. c – 239
5. c – 219	22. b – 229	39. b – 240
6. c – 219	23. c – 230	40. d – 241
7. a – 220	24. c – 231	41. b – 241
8. d – 220	25. a – 232	42. b – 242
9. b – 221	26. b – 232	43. b – 242
10. b – 221	27. a – 232	44. a – 242
11. b – 221	28. a – 233	45. c – 243
12. c – 221	29. c – 233	46. c – 245
13. d – 223	30. b – 234	47. c – 245
14. b – 223	31. c – 235	48. b – 246
15. b – 224	32. a – 236	49. a – 247
16. b – 225	33. d – 237	50. b – 248
17. c – 225	34. c – 237	

Answer Key: CHAPTER 8 — Skin Physiology

1. d – 259	18. b – 267	35. a – 285
2. d – 259	19. a – 268	36. d – 286
3. a – 259	20. d – 269	37. b – 287
4. d – 260	21. d – 269	38. a – 287
5. c – 260	22. d – 269	39. b – 289
6. b – 261	23. a – 270	40. a – 290
7. b – 262	24. b – 273	41. c – 290
8. d – 262	25. a – 275	42. a – 291
9. c – 262	26. a – 275	43. c – 291
10. b – 263	27. c – 276	44. b – 291
11. b – 264	28. b – 277	45. b – 292
12. c – 264	29. a – 278	46. a – 292
13. d – 265	30. c – 278	47. b – 292
14. a – 265	31. b – 280	48. b – 292
15. a – 266	32. c – 281	49. d – 292
16. c – 267	33. d – 282	50. c – 292
17. a – 267	34. c – 283	

Answer Key: CHAPTER 9 — Client Care

1. b – 300	11. b – 306	21. c – 309
2. c – 300	12. c – 306	22. d – 313
3. b – 301	13. d – 306	23. d – 314
4. b – 301	14. d – 307	24. b – 315
5. a – 303	15. c – 307	25. c – 316
6. c – 304	16. b – 307	26. c – 316
7. a – 304	17. c – 307	27. b – 317
8. c – 305	18. d – 308	28. a – 317
9. b – 305	19. d – 308	29. b – 317
10. d – 305	20. c – 309	30. c – 318

Answer Key: CHAPTER 10 — Facials

1. d – 325	15. a – 330	29. a – 333
2. b – 325	16. d – 330	30. d – 334
3. b – 326	17. b – 331	31. b – 335
4. c – 326	18. d – 331	32. c – 337
5. d – 327	19. b – 331	33. a – 337
6. c – 327	20. c – 332	34. d – 338
7. c – 327	21. b – 332	35. a – 338
8. b – 328	22. c – 333	36. b – 343
9. d – 328	23. a – 333	37. d – 346
10. c – 328	24. a – 333	38. c – 351
11. a – 329	25. d – 333	39. d – 352
12. d – 329	26. c – 333	40. d – 360
13. b – 330	27. c – 333	
14. c – 330	28. b – 333	

Answer Key: CHAPTER 11 — Hair Removal

1. c – 371	16. b – 373	31. d – 376
2. b – 372	17. b – 373	32. b – 376
3. d – 372	18. b – 373	33. c – 377
4. b – 372	19. c – 373	34. d – 377
5. c – 372	20. c – 374	35. a – 377
6. a – 372	21. a – 375	36. a – 377
7. d – 372	22. c – 375	37. d – 377
8. b – 372	23. d – 375	38. a – 377
9. a – 372	24. a – 376	39. d – 377
10. c – 372	25. c – 376	40. a – 380
11. d – 372	26. b – 376	41. c – 380
12. b – 372	27. c – 376	42. c – 382
13. c – 372	28. b – 376	43. d – 383
14. a – 372	29. d – 376	44. b – 383
15. b – 373	30. b – 376	45. c – 387

Answer Key: CHAPTER 12 — Makeup

1. c – 409	16. a – 412	31. b – 424
2. d – 409	17. c – 413	32. a – 424
3. a – 409	18. a – 414	33. b – 426
4. b – 409	19. b – 415	34. a – 427
5. d – 409	20. c – 416	35. c – 431
6. b – 409	21. a – 417	36. d – 431
7. d – 410	22. d – 418	37. a – 435
8. c – 410	23. d – 418	38. c – 435
9. c – 410	24. a – 419	39. a – 435
10. a – 410	25. b – 419	40. d – 435
11. d – 410	26. b – 419	41. b – 437
12. b – 410	27. c – 420	42. a – 437
13. a – 411	28. a – 421	43. b – 441
14. d – 411	29. b – 421	44. c – 456
15. b – 411	30. a – 422	45. c – 459

Answer Key: CHAPTER 13 — Advanced Treatments

1. c – 465	16. a – 486	31. c – 496
2. a – 466	17. c – 487	32. d – 497
3. b – 466	18. d – 488	33. a – 499
4. a – 469	19. c – 490	34. d – 499
5. d – 472	20. b – 493	35. c – 499
6. d – 472	21. c – 494	36. d – 499
7. b – 475	22. a – 495	37. c – 500
8. c – 477	23. c – 495	38. d – 500
9. b – 479	24. b – 495	39. a – 500
10. c – 482	25. c – 495	40. d – 500
11. b – 482	26. d – 495	41. d – 501
12. c – 482	27. a – 495	42. c – 501
13. b – 482	28. a – 496	43. d – 501
14. c – 484	29. b – 496	44. b – 502
15. c – 484	30. b – 496	45. d – 502

Answer Key: CHAPTER 14 — Estheticians in the Medical Field

1. d – 510	16. c – 516	31. a – 520
2. d – 510	17. b – 516	32. b – 520
3. b – 511	18. a – 516	33. c – 520
4. d – 511	19. d – 516	34. c – 520
5. c – 511	20. d – 517	35. d – 520
6. d – 511	21. a – 517	36. d – 520
7. d – 512	22. a – 517	37. a – 521
8. d – 512	23. b – 517	38. d – 521
9. b – 513	24. d – 519	39. c – 521
10. c – 513	25. b – 519	40. c – 521
11. a – 513	26. d – 519	41. b – 521
12. b – 514	27. b – 519	42. b – 521
13. d – 515	28. b – 519	43. d – 521
14. c – 515	29. c – 520	44. d – 524
15. c – 516	30. b – 520	45. b – 524

Answer Key: FINAL EXAM

1. c – 3	35. b – 180	69. a – 330
2. b – 5	36. c – 183	70. c – 333
3. d – 5	37. a – 187	71. b – 333
4. d – 5	38. b – 190	72. b – 335
5. d – 18	39. a – 195	73. d – 346
6. a – 35	40. c – 211	74. d – 372
7. b – 44	41. a – 218	75. c – 372
8. c – 48	42. a – 218	76. d – 372
9. b – 52	43. b – 221	77. c – 374
10. b – 52	44. b – 225	78. a – 375
11. d – 72	45. c – 226	79. a – 377
12. a – 74	46. c – 233	80. d – 377
13. c – 78	47. c – 235	81. d – 383
14. d – 80	48. d – 237	82. d – 409
15. b – 84	49. b – 242	83. d – 410
16. a – 92	50. a – 247	84. a – 411
17. b – 99	51. d – 259	85. a – 419
18. c – 104	52. b – 261	86. b – 424
19. d – 105	53. d – 265	87. a – 435
20. d – 107	54. a – 267	88. b – 441
21. c – 112	55. d – 269	89. d – 466
22. d – 115	56. a – 275	90. b – 482
23. d – 118	57. d – 283	91. b – 495
24. d – 126	58. b – 290	92. c – 496
25. a – 131	59. d – 292	93. c – 499
26. a – 132	60. c – 294	94. a – 502
27. d – 134	61. b – 300	95. d – 510
28. b – 134	62. c – 307	96. c – 513
29. b – 143	63. c – 309	97. d – 515
30. d – 153	64. c – 316	98. b – 519
31. c – 159	65. d – 318	99. b – 520
32. b – 169	66. d – 325	100. b – 524
33. b – 175	67. c – 327	
34. d – 177	68. a – 329	

Did You Know? CHAPTER 1 — Personal Development

Check the box if you know the material.

- ☐ 1. To function properly most people need six to eight hours of sleep per night.
- ☐ 2. Overexertion and lack of sleep deplete the body's vitality.
- ☐ 3. A well balanced exercise routine includes cardiorespiratory activities, strength training and flexibility.
- ☐ 4. Stress is managed by maintaining moderation and balance.
- ☐ 5. Anger can cause the heart rate to increase.
- ☐ 6. RDA refers to Recommended Dietary Allowances.
- ☐ 7. The energy contained in food is measured in calories.
- ☐ 8. Carbohydrates, proteins and fats are energy-producing substances contained in almost all foods.
- ☐ 9. Carbohydrates account for the greatest percentage of your daily nutrient intake.
- ☐ 10. Other essential nutrients include water, vitamins and minerals.
- ☐ 11. Hygiene is the applied science that deals with healthful living.
- ☐ 12. Public hygiene is promoting and preserving the health of the community.
- ☐ 13. Bathing regularly with soap and using deodorant are examples of personal hygiene.
- ☐ 14. Halitosis refers to bad breath.
- ☐ 15. Good oral hygiene maintains healthy teeth and gums and prevents bad breath.
- ☐ 16. The nails of an esthetician should be attractively manicured and short.
- ☐ 17. Good posture and wearing properly fitted, low broad-heeled shoes give the body support and balance.

- ☐ 18. Clothing for an esthetician should be simplistic.
- ☐ 19. Good posture reduces fatigue and helps internal organs function properly.
- ☐ 20. Ergonomics is the study of the relationship between people and their work environment.
- ☐ 21. Varicose veins refers to swollen veins.
- ☐ 22. Carpal Tunnel Syndrome numbs and weakens the hands and can affect the ability to work.
- ☐ 23. When sitting in a chair, keep your back straight.
- ☐ 24. The exchange of messages without speaking is nonverbal communication.
- ☐ 25. The level and tone of voice, inflection and rate of speech are important in verbal communication.
- ☐ 26. The use of poor grammar makes intended messages unclear.
- ☐ 27. Handling clients with tact is important in building professional relationships.
- ☐ 28. Active listening involves the whole body.
- ☐ 29. Reflective listening is repeating out loud what was heard, processed and reported.
- ☐ 30. The suggested topic of conversation with a client is the client's lifestyle and beauty needs.
- ☐ 31. An esthetician should handle a complaint calmly and judiciously.
- ☐ 32. Personality is the outward reflection of inner feelings, thoughts, attitudes and values.
- ☐ 33. Friendliness, a positive attitude and vitality are all part of a pleasing personality.
- ☐ 34. An attitude is a feeling or emotion and can be changed.
- ☐ 35. Habits are learned behaviors reinforced through events in the environment.

Did You Know? CHAPTER 2 — Professional Development
Check the box if you know the material.

☐ 1. A resumé is a one- or two-page outline that describes personal and professional attributes in a brief, concise manner.

☐ 2. White, ivory (pale beige), pale blue or pale gray paper is recommended for resumés.

☐ 3. Professional resumé writers recommend using a non-decorative, simple 10 to 11 point font.

☐ 4. A cover letter is the companion piece to a resumé that introduces you to the prospective employer.

☐ 5. Simply styled hair presents a professional image at a job interview.

☐ 6. The size of the skin care center is considered to be the least important factor in deciding whether to accept a position.

☐ 7. A common practice with companies is to have new employees complete a general orientation program and apprenticeship.

☐ 8. Networking is developing relationships with individuals who can put you in contact with potential customers or employers.

☐ 9. Customer service is personal attention to the needs of the client.

☐ 10. Word-of-mouth advertising is the most effective way to build your clientele.

☐ 11. Asking clients to rebook before they leave the skin care center is a simple and effective technique for building clientele.

☐ 12. Retailing is recommending and providing the best products for client purchase.

☐ 13. Successful estheticians effectively prescribe their services along with the appropriate skin care products for home care.

☐ 14. Features of a product include its characteristics, such as the size of the container, the aroma or a specific ingredient.

☐ 15. Benefits of a product are what a product will do to enhance the appearance or improve the condition of the client's skin.

☐ 16. Cross-selling is building on a sale by recommending a product that complements another product the client has already purchased.

☐ 17. The esthetician should examine the client's skin condition regularly to determine the continued effectiveness of recommended products and home care.

☐ 18. Need is the easiest buyer motivation to recognize.

☐ 19. Displaying a minimum of two products on the front edge of a display shelf creating easy access and high visibility of the products is called facing the product.

☐ 20. Comparison shopping is the practice of visiting competitors to compare their business practices to your own.

Did You Know? CHAPTER 3 — Business Basics

Check the box if you know the material.

☐ 1. A business plan is the central company document that the owner and employees use to make decisions.

☐ 2. Assets, liabilities and net worth are the three basic elements of a personal financial statement.

☐ 3. On a personal financial statement, all the money owed is called liabilities.

☐ 4. Assets minus liabilities equals net worth.

☐ 5. A sole proprietorship is a business owned by one person who is in complete control of the business.

☐ 6. A business owned by two or more persons is called a partnership.

☐ 7. A corporation is owned by its shareholders.

☐ 8. An accountant is a financial advisor who sets up a basic bookkeeping system and reviews rental agreements.

☐ 9. A lawyer is the advisor on borrowing money, signing rental agreements and assuming tax responsibilities.

☐ 10. The distributor acts as a link between the manufacturer and the skin care center.

☐ 11. The most important factor in opening a skin care business is location.

☐ 12. Determining how many skin care centers are in the area is the first step in gauging the market need.

☐ 13. An efficient working space allows for 120 to 150 square feet per esthetician.

☐ 14. Operating capital is the reservoir of cash that is needed to stay ahead of creditors.

☐ 15. A line of credit, from the bank is a reserve of cash that you can draw upon to meet operating expenses if you have a slow month or two.

☐ 16. Fixed rent allows owners to predict monthly expenses carefully.

- ☐ 17. Variable rent is a set dollar amount paid per month plus a percentage of the total monthly income.
- ☐ 18. Insurance is a type of risk management.
- ☐ 19. Malpractice insurance covers the cost of a lawsuit or settlement resulting from damage inflicted on a client during any service.
- ☐ 20. Property insurance covers the actual skin care center equipment and physical location in case of natural disasters.
- ☐ 21. Worker's compensation is required by law.
- ☐ 22. Income refers to all payments received from clients for services performed and home care products purchased.
- ☐ 23. Operating expenses are all costs incurred in the day-to-day running of the skin care center.
- ☐ 24. Variable costs include utilities, supplies, cost of promotions, postage and taxes.
- ☐ 25. If a skin care center's income is greater than operating expenses, the skin care center is operating at a profit.
- ☐ 26. A projection is an estimate of what will be earned in revenues and what will be paid out in expenses.
- ☐ 27. Social Security tax is a withholding tax that is a planned savings/retirement fund for every worker in the United States.
- ☐ 28. A skin care center owner must apply for a State Sales Tax Permit before collecting tax on products or services sold.
- ☐ 29. A skin care center should keep all records of daily sales and services for at least six months.
- ☐ 30. Commission is based on a percentage of the dollar income the individual esthetician generates by serving clients.

Did You Know? CHAPTER 4 — Skin Care Center Ecology

Check the box if you know the material.

☐ 1. Microbiology is the study of small living organisms called microbes.

☐ 2. Bacteria are one-celled microorganisms that are classified as either disease-producing or nondisease-producing.

☐ 3. Nonpathogenic bacteria are nondisease-producing bacteria.

☐ 4. Saprophytes are nonpathogenic bacteria that live on dead matter.

☐ 5. Cocci are spherical or round-shaped bacterial cells that appear singularly or in groups.

☐ 6. Staphylococci are pus-forming bacterial cells that are present in abscesses, pustules and boils.

☐ 7. Diplococci are bacterial cells that grow in pairs and cause pneumonia.

☐ 8. Bacilli are the most common form of bacterial cells.

☐ 9. Bacteria reproduce and grow rapidly during the active stage of the growth cycle.

☐ 10. The normal dormant stage that bacteria enter when the environment makes the bacteria's survival difficult is called the inactive stage.

☐ 11. Bacilli and spirilla are able to move themselves by using hair-like projections known as flagella.

☐ 12. A sub-microscopic infectious agent that replicates itself only within cells of living hosts is called a virus.

☐ 13. HBV is a highly infectious disease that affects the liver.

☐ 14. Acquired Immunodeficiency Syndrome (AIDS) is a highly infectious disease that interferes with the body's natural immune system.

☐ 15. Head lice, itch mites, ringworm and nail fungus are all diseases caused by external parasites.

☐ 16. The growth of a parasitic organism within the body is known as an infection.

☐ 17. Bloodborne pathogens are bacteria or viruses that are transmitted through blood or body fluids causing infectious diseases.

☐ 18. Tuberculosis is a contagious, potentially fatal infection caused by airborne bacteria that first affect the lungs.

☐ 19. A contagious disease refers to a disease that is easily spread from one person to another.

☐ 20. An infection present in a small, confined area indicated by a pus-filled boil, pimple or inflammation is a local infection.

☐ 21. A boil, pimple or inflammation are all examples of local infections.

☐ 22. Immunity is the body's ability to destroy infectious agents that enter it.

☐ 23. Passive immunity is the stimulation of the body's immune response through the injection of antigens.

☐ 24. Efforts to prevent the spread of disease and kill microbes are referred as infection control.

☐ 25. Infection control procedures are divided into three levels of sanitation, disinfection and sterilization.

☐ 26. Hives, itching and swelling all indicate an allergic reaction to latex.

☐ 27. Sanitation is the lowest level of infection control.

☐ 28. Antiseptics are products used to arrest or prevent the growth of microorganisms on the skin.

☐ 29. Efficacy labels are required on all disinfectants and inform the user about what organisms the product is effective against.

☐ 30. Washing your hands with a liquid antibacterial soap and water is an example of procedures used during sanitation.

☐ 31. The second level of infection control that does not eliminate bacterial spores is called disinfection.

☐ 32. Instruments can be pre-cleaned using high-frequency energy waves.

☐ 33. The 2001 OSHA Bloodborne Pathogens Standard requires the use of an EPA-registered disinfectant.

☐ 34. OSHA is the regulating agency that enforces safety and health standards in the workplace.

☐ 35. A Material Safety Data Sheet (MSDS) provides key information that may prove helpful during an allergic reaction related to product usage.

☐ 36. Key information on a specific product regarding ingredients, associated hazards, combustion levels and storage requirements is provided by the MSDS.

☐ 37. Sponges and disposable files are porous products used in the skin care center that cannot be properly disinfected.

☐ 38. A covered container is required for storage of disinfected implements.

☐ 39. The process referred to as "double-bagging" is performed when a blood spill occurs.

☐ 40. It is important to wear gloves to protect your skin when mixing chemical disinfecting agents.

☐ 41. The level of infection control that destroys all small organisms, including bacterial spores, is called sterilization.

☐ 42. Tools and instruments used to puncture or invade the skin must be sterilized or disposable.

☐ 43. A UV light sterilizer machine uses UV light to kill bacteria in a dry setting.

☐ 44. A steam autoclave machine uses pressurized steam to sterilize critical implements.

☐ 45. A chemiclave sterilizes surgical instruments with high-pressure, high-temperature vapor.

☐ 46. A bleeding wound should be treated by covering the wound and applying pressure.

☐ 47. An electrical burn is usually the result of faulty equipment or improper use of equipment.

☐ 48. Determining if the victim can talk or cough is the first course of action taken if it is suspected that a client is choking.

☐ 49. If a fainting victim does not regain consciousness immediately, the esthetician should call 9-1-1.

☐ 50. Steps taken in the event of a cut, scratch or embedded object in the eye are: place a gauze pad or cloth over both eyes, secure a gauze pad or cloth with a bandage and get to an eye specialist or emergency room immediately.

Did You Know? CHAPTER 5 — Anatomy

Check the box if you know the material.

☐ 1. Anatomy is the study of the organs and systems of the body.

☐ 2. The basic structure of a cell consists of a nucleus, cytoplasm and the cell membrane.

☐ 3. Cells are the basic units of life.

☐ 4. The nucleus is the control center of cell activities.

☐ 5. Cytoplasm is the production department of the cell.

☐ 6. Human cells reproduce by a process referred to as mitosis.

☐ 7. Metabolism is the chemical process by which cells receive nutrients for cell growth and reproduction.

☐ 8. Anabolism is the process of building up larger molecules from smaller ones.

☐ 9. Catabolism causes a release of energy within the cell.

☐ 10. Tissues are groups of cells of the same kind.

☐ 11. Nerve tissue carries messages to and from the brain and coordinates body functions.

☐ 12. The skin, brain and stomach are all organs of the body. The hands are not an organ of the body.

☐ 13. When stimulated, muscular tissue contracts to produce motion.

☐ 14. Organs are separate body structures that perform specific functions.

☐ 15. A system is a group of body structures that perform one or more vital functions for the body.

☐ 16. Nervous, digestive and circulatory are all body systems.

☐ 17. The skeletal system is the physical foundation of the body.

☐ 18. Osteology is the study of bones.

☐ 19. Flat bones are plate-shaped bones located in the skull, scapula, hip bone, sternum, ribs and according to some, the patella.

- ☐ 20. The skull is the facial skeleton that encloses and protects the brain and primary sensory organs.
- ☐ 21. The frontal bone extends from the top of the eyes to the top of the head to form the forehead.
- ☐ 22. The parietal bones form the crown and upper sides of the head.
- ☐ 23. Nine of the 14 bones that compose the facial skeleton are involved in facial massage.
- ☐ 24. The mandible is the lower jaw and the largest bone of the facial skeleton.
- ☐ 25. The cervical vertebrae are the seven bones that form the top part of the spinal column.
- ☐ 26. The spine, sternum and 12 ribs make up the thorax.
- ☐ 27. Phalanges are the 14 bones that form the fingers.
- ☐ 28. Levator is the term used to describe a muscle that lifts up.
- ☐ 29. Cardiac, voluntary and involuntary are all types of muscle tissue.
- ☐ 30. Voluntary muscles respond to conscious commands.
- ☐ 31. Non-striated muscles respond automatically to control various body functions.
- ☐ 32. The three parts of the muscle are the origin, belly and insertion.
- ☐ 33. Tendons are bands of fibrous tissue that attach the muscle to the bones.
- ☐ 34. Muscles affected by massage are generally manipulated from the insertion to the origin.
- ☐ 35. The epicranius is a broad muscle that covers the scalp.
- ☐ 36. The occipitalis is a muscle located at the back of the neck and draws the scalp back.
- ☐ 37. The procerus draws brows down and wrinkles the area across the bridge of the nose.
- ☐ 38. The zygomaticus draws the mouth up and back, as in laughing or smiling.

☐ 39. The buccinator is responsible for compressing the cheek to release air outwardly, as in blowing.

☐ 40. The mastication muscle that is located above and in front of the ear, and performs both opening and closing of the jaw, is the temporalis.

☐ 41. The sternocleido mastoideus causes the head to move from side to side and up and down.

☐ 42. The supinator turns the palm of the hand up.

☐ 43. The flexor ulnaris is located mid-forearm and bends the wrist and closes the fingers.

☐ 44. The abductor muscles separate the fingers.

☐ 45. Opponens muscles cause the thumb to move toward the fingers, giving the ability to grasp or make a fist.

☐ 46. The circulatory system controls the circulation of blood and lymph through the body.

☐ 47. The heart, arteries, veins and capillaries are all a part of the cardiovascular system.

☐ 48. The heart is entirely encased in a membrane called the pericardium.

☐ 49. The lower chambers of the heart consist of the right ventricle and left ventricle.

☐ 50. The normal heart beats about 60-80 times per minute.

☐ 51. Blood is transported through veins, arteries and capillaries.

☐ 52. White blood cells fight bacteria and other foreign substances and increase in number when infection invades the body.

☐ 53. The process of coagulation is started by thrombocytes.

☐ 54. Plasma is the fluid part of the blood in which red and white blood cells and blood platelets are suspended.

☐ 55. Arteries carry oxygenated blood away from the heart through the body.

- [ ] 56. Systemic circulation is the process of blood traveling from the heart throughout the body and back to the heart.
- [ ] 57. The common carotid arteries supply blood to the head, face and neck.
- [ ] 58. The internal carotid artery supplies blood to the brain, eyes and forehead.
- [ ] 59. All blood from the head, face and neck returns through the internal jugular and external jugular veins.
- [ ] 60. Wearing support hose and the correctly sized shoes can prevent varicose veins.
- [ ] 61. The external maxillary supplies the lower portion of the face with blood.
- [ ] 62. Lymph nodes act as barriers to infection from one part of the body to another.
- [ ] 63. The nervous system coordinates and controls the overall operation of the human body by responding to both internal and external stimuli.
- [ ] 64. The brain controls all three subsystems of the nervous system.
- [ ] 65. The medulla oblongata is considered the most vital part of the brain containing centers that control breathing and heart function.
- [ ] 66. Primary components of the nervous system include the brain, spinal cord and nerves.
- [ ] 67. The central nervous system is composed of the brain and spinal cord.
- [ ] 68. The peripheral nervous system carries sensory information to the brain by the ears, eyes, nose and tongue.
- [ ] 69. The autonomic nervous system is responsible for all involuntary body functions.
- [ ] 70. The parasympathetic nervous system is the sub-system of the autonomic system which slows the heart rate, dilates blood vessels and lowers blood pressure.

- ☐ 71. Homeostasis describes the body's state of balance.
- ☐ 72. Axons are long and short threadlike fibers that extend from nerve cells.
- ☐ 73. Nerve terminals are responsible for sending messages in the form of nerve impulses.
- ☐ 74. The interaction of sensory and motor nerves is called a reflex action.
- ☐ 75. Motor, sensory and sensory-motor are all types of nerves.
- ☐ 76. Motor nerves carry messages from the brain to the muscles and cause a muscle to react.
- ☐ 77. Mixed nerves perform both sensory and motor functions.
- ☐ 78. Receptors are nerve cells that react to outside stimulation by sending a sensory message to the brain.
- ☐ 79. The eleventh cranial nerve that controls the motion of the neck muscles is the accessory nerve.
- ☐ 80. The trifacial nerve is the chief sensory nerve of the face responsible for transmitting facial sensations to the brain and controlling the muscle movements of chewing.
- ☐ 81. The trifacial nerve controls sensations of the face, teeth and tongue.
- ☐ 82. The three branches of the trifacial nerve are maxillary, ophthalmic and mandibular.
- ☐ 83. The main nerve branch to the top 1/3 of the face is the ophthalmic branch.
- ☐ 84. The zygomatic nerve extends to the side of the forehead, temple and upper part of the cheek.
- ☐ 85. The auriculo temporal nerve extends to the ear and to the area from the top of the head to the temple.
- ☐ 86. The seventh cranial nerve and primary motor nerve of the face is the facial nerve.

- ☐ 87. The cervical branch of the facial nerve extends to the muscles on the side of the neck.
- ☐ 88. The temporal branch extends to the muscles of the temple, the side of the forehead, the eyebrow, eyelid and upper cheek.
- ☐ 89. The radial nerve extends down the thumb side of the arm into the back of the hand.
- ☐ 90. The digestive system breaks food down into simpler chemical compounds that can be easily absorbed by cells or eliminated from the body as waste.
- ☐ 91. The stomach, pharynx and esophagus are all parts of the digestive system.
- ☐ 92. Enzymes are secreted by salivary glands to break down food.
- ☐ 93. The excretory system eliminates solid, liquid and gaseous waste products from the body.
- ☐ 94. The skin, liver and kidneys are all organs of the excretory system.
- ☐ 95. The skin is the body's largest organ.
- ☐ 96. The liver converts and neutralizes ammonia from the circulatory system to urea.
- ☐ 97. The lower respiratory tract consists of the lungs, trachea and bronchi.
- ☐ 98. The endocrine system is a carefully balanced mechanism that directly affects hair growth, skin conditions and energy levels.
- ☐ 99. The skin and its layers make up the integumentary system.
- ☐ 100. The two primary glands of the integumentary system are the sebaceous and sudoriferous.

Did You Know? CHAPTER 6 — Electricity and Electrical Equipment

Check the box if you know the material.

☐ 1. Light, heat, chemical and magnetic changes are all produced by electricity.

☐ 2. The flow of electrons moving along a conductor is an electric current.

☐ 3. The electric current in which electrons move at an even rate and flow only in one direction is called a direct current.

☐ 4. A rapid, oscillating cycle that alternates back and forth allowing electrons to flow first in one direction and then in the other is an alternating current.

☐ 5. A hertz rating is the number of cycles per second that a generator alternates current.

☐ 6. Material that easily transports electricity is a conductor.

☐ 7. Materials that do not allow electricity to flow through them are called insulators.

☐ 8. Amps, volts, watts and ohms are all units that measure electricity.

☐ 9. One ampere equals 1,000 milliamperes.

☐ 10. A volt is a unit of electric pressure.

☐ 11. A unit of electrical resistance is called an ohm.

☐ 12. Appliances should be turned off, unplugged, and stored in a safe place when not in use.

☐ 13. A path in which electricity travels is a closed circuit.

☐ 14. Load is the technical term for any appliance that requires electricity in order to work.

☐ 15. More current flowing through a line than it is designed to carry is called an overload.

☐ 16. In the event of a fire from electrical overload, turn off the circuit, use a fire extinguisher rated for electrical fires or call the fire department if the fire is beyond your control.

☐ 17. A short circuit can occur any time a foreign conductor comes in contact with a wire carrying current to a load.

☐ 18. Wear rubber gloves, turn off main power, and unplug equipment from the power source when installing a fuse.

☐ 19. Two metal pieces that make contact with each other to allow the flow of electric current are found on a circuit breaker.

☐ 20. A safety device designed to protect the user during the operation of appliances is a grounding wire.

☐ 21. Local shock passes through the body and can cause burns.

☐ 22. The type of shock causing the heart to stop, breathing to cease and muscles to convulse is referred to as a general shock.

☐ 23. Posting local fire codes, inspecting fire safety devices and storing flammable materials properly are all protocols of fire prevention.

☐ 24. The direct current used in electrotherapy treatments is Galvanic.

☐ 25. Anaphoresis is a type of phoresis often used in desincrustation.

☐ 26. Iontophoresis treatment uses cataphoresis to build up or nourish the deeper layers of the epidermis.

☐ 27. Having opposite poles in an electrical current is referred to as polarity.

☐ 28. The negatively charged electrode is called a cathode.

- ☐ 29. An anode is a positively charged electrode.
- ☐ 30. When performing a treatment using Galvanic Current, and the electrode held by the esthetician is in the positive mode, the reaction on the skin will be acidic.
- ☐ 31. Tesla, a High Frequency current, is also known as the violet ray.
- ☐ 32. Benefits of Direct High Frequency include: stimulates surface tissue, heals existing papules and pustules and increases circulation and blood flow.
- ☐ 33. A narrow space between the electrode and skin used to provide germicidal, healing and drying effects during either Direct or Indirect High Frequency treatments is a spark gap.
- ☐ 34. Faradic Current is used chiefly to cause muscle contractions.
- ☐ 35. An alternating current that penetrates more deeply and can provide greater stimulation to the treated area than a Faradic Current is called Sinusoidal.
- ☐ 36. Pregnancy, epilepsy, diabetes or other conditions that suggest it is inadvisable to perform a procedure on a client is a contraindication.
- ☐ 37. White light is a combination light that can be broken into its individual wavelengths by a prism.
- ☐ 38. Bacteria that cause skin infections can be killed by ultraviolet light.
- ☐ 39. UVA rays are most frequently used in tanning booths.
- ☐ 40. The transfer of heat via direct contact is conduction.
- ☐ 41. Rotating brushes produce mechanical effects.
- ☐ 42. Electric current that travels through a water-based solution and onto the body has an electrochemical effect.

☐ 43. The Wood's Lamp is a type of electrical equipment that uses violet rays or black light to analyze skin type and condition.

☐ 44. A device that sprays a lukewarm, diffused vapor mist onto the surface of the facial skin is called a facial steamer.

☐ 45. Rosacea, sensitive skin and couperose skin are contraindications for using steam machines.

Did You Know? CHAPTER 7 — Chemistry
Check the box if you know the material.

☐ 1. Inorganic chemistry is the study of the elements in the Periodic Table and their compounds except the compounds based on carbon.

☐ 2. Matter is anything that occupies space.

☐ 3. Liquids have definite weight and volume and take the shape of the container in which they are poured.

☐ 4. Gases are matter with definite weight, but indefinite volume and shape.

☐ 5. A chemical change is a change in substance that creates a new substance with different material characteristics from those of the original substance.

☐ 6. When a physical change occurs, chemical structure does not change and changes always involve either the gain or loss of energy. Freezing water to form ice cubes is an example of a physical change.

☐ 7. Periodic law is the unifying concept used to organize elements and their similarities.

☐ 8. The Periodic Table of Chemical Elements was created by Dmitri Mendeleev and Lothar Meyer to arrange the elements, includes 92 naturally occurring elements and uses atomic numbers as the primary basis for organization.

☐ 9. Oxygen is the most abundant element in the earth's crust.

☐ 10. Protons have a positive electrical charge and identify the atom.

☐ 11. The molecular weight of each element is determined by the protons and neutrons.

☐ 12. Electrons have a negative electrical charge.

☐ 13. A compound is created by chemically uniting two different elements.

☐ 14. Compounds are formed by the union of individual elements, held together by forces called chemical bonds, and more than four million have been identified.

- ☐ 15. Reduction is a process in which a substance gains an electron and oxygen is released.
- ☐ 16. Biochemistry is the branch of science that deals with the chemicals related to life processes and their reactions within the body.
- ☐ 17. Enzymes are materials that dissolve and break down large molecules into smaller ones.
- ☐ 18. Amino acids consist of carbon, oxygen, hydrogen and nitrogen and join together in chains to form proteins. There are 22 common amino acids.
- ☐ 19. Carbohydrates play a key role in metabolism and are used by the body to store energy. Glucose is the most important carbohydrate for providing energy.
- ☐ 20. A saccharide is a simple unit of a carbohydrate.
- ☐ 21. The term alkaline is used to describe a base product.
- ☐ 22. The average pH range of the skin is 4.5 to 5.5.
- ☐ 23. The acid mantle is a mixture of sebum and sweat combined with lipids, minerals and moisture to form a protective barrier for the skin.
- ☐ 24. You can keep your client's skin in top shape by treating each client with products that balance the individual's pH, reading labels knowledgeably, and by selecting and recommending the right product for home care.
- ☐ 25. The solute is the solid, or dissolved part, of a solution.
- ☐ 26. The saturation point is the point at which a solute will no longer dissolve evenly in the solvent.
- ☐ 27. Solvents that easily mix together are called miscible.
- ☐ 28. A stick is a hard, low-level water or anhydrous product used by rubbing the product directly on the skin.
- ☐ 29. Aerosols are explosive and flammable, packaged under pressure and blended with a propellant inside a container.
- ☐ 30. An emulsifier is compatible with both water and oil.

☐ 31. Active ingredients are responsible for producing the desired effect.

☐ 32. Water is the first ingredient found in the majority of cosmetic skin care products.

☐ 33. Humectants are organic ingredients that bind water and deposit it onto the skin.

☐ 34. Emollients are used to condition and soften the skin, provide a protective barrier called an occlusive barrier and help the skin maintain its natural hydration by sealing moisture in the skin.

☐ 35. Surfactants have the ability to bind a wide range of organic and inorganic matter to water.

☐ 36. Thickeners allow for the suspension of small particle solids in a base by creating a supporting structure to prevent settling.

☐ 37. Botanicals are able to produce conditioning effects, antibacterial effects and anti-inflammatory effects.

☐ 38. Preservatives are included in cosmetic products to maintain microbiological integrity or product quality during production, storage and use by the consumer.

☐ 39. Coloring agents are vegetable, mineral or pigment dyes that are added to products to enhance the product's appearance.

☐ 40. The term hypoallergenic means that the product is less likely to provoke an allergic reaction.

☐ 41. Fragrance is an ingredient used in skin care products to cover (mask) undesirable odors in the product base.

☐ 42. Acids or bases used to adjust the desired product pH level are called pH adjustors.

☐ 43. Comedogenic ingredients are likely to block or clog the pores and contribute to pimples.

☐ 44. Sunscreens are products used to block or absorb ultraviolet radiation emitted by the sun, considered drugs under FDA guidelines and usually 2% to 7% in concentration.

☐ 45. Free radicals are chemically unstable molecules caused by environmental pollutants and UV exposure.

☐ 46. Cyclomethicone is a non-comedogenic emollient that gives a product a silky feel.

☐ 47. Hydroxy acids are organic acids extracted from a variety of natural sources such as fruits, sugar and milk.

☐ 48. Enzymes are ingredients that are designed to dissolve keratin proteins on the surface of the skin.

☐ 49. Lighteners slowly block the production of melanin in the skin, bleach or lighten areas of hyperpigmentation and usually take months of continued use to deliver a noticeable effect.

☐ 50. The FTC regulates the promotion and advertising of cosmetics and many other products.

Did You Know? CHAPTER 8 — Skin Physiology

Check the box if you know the material.

- ☐ 1. The study of the skin's functions is referred to as skin physiology.
- ☐ 2. Functions of the skin include secretion, protection and absorption.
- ☐ 3. Pores are tiny openings that allow sweat or sebum to pass through the surface of the skin.
- ☐ 4. Immune cells provide the body with its first line of defense against infection by identifying foreign substances in the skin.
- ☐ 5. Sebum is a complex mixture of fatty acids that keeps the skin soft, supple and pliable.
- ☐ 6. Main layers of the skin include the dermal layer, epidermal layer and subcutaneous layer.
- ☐ 7. The epidermis is known as the skin's protective layer.
- ☐ 8. The epidermis is composed primarily of keratinocytes.
- ☐ 9. The stratum corneum is the toughest layer of the epidermis.
- ☐ 10. Desmosomes are intercellular connections that allow keratinocytes on the surface of the skin to remain tightly interconnected.
- ☐ 11. "Spiny" irregularly shaped cells are located in the stratum spinosum.
- ☐ 12. The stratum granulosum is the layer of the skin in which the cells are more regularly shaped and resemble many tiny granules.
- ☐ 13. Collagen is a strong protein substance that, when broken down, forms bundles that strengthen and give structure to the skin.
- ☐ 14. The dermis is referred to as the "true skin."
- ☐ 15. Krause's end bulbs, Ruffini's corpuscles and Meissner's corpuscles are all receptors of sensation in the dermal layer of the skin.
- ☐ 16. Sudoriferous glands produce sweat.

- ☐ 17. Apocrine glands are located on the nipples, genitals and underarms.
- ☐ 18. Eccrine glands are most abundant on the forehead, soles of the feet and palms of the hands.
- ☐ 19. Androgen is a male hormone that influences the production of sebum.
- ☐ 20. The subcutaneous layer is the structure that insulates and acts as a shock absorber to protect the bones.
- ☐ 21. Ligaments hold bones to other bones to form joints.
- ☐ 22. Nervous tissue, muscular tissue and connective tissue are all forms of tissue found in the skin.
- ☐ 23. Pain receptors, thermoreceptors and Pacinian corpuscles are all types of sensory cells.
- ☐ 24. Exfoliation is the removal of dead skin cells to stimulate new cell growth.
- ☐ 25. Hydration level, oiliness of the skin and temperature of the skin are all factors of skin absorption.
- ☐ 26. A lesion is a change in the structure of skin tissue.
- ☐ 27. Crust, a type of secondary lesion, is a dried mass that is the remains of an oozing sore.
- ☐ 28. Atopic dermatitis is a hereditary rash, or inflammation of the skin, characterized by dry, sensitive irritated skin.
- ☐ 29. Hives is an allergic reaction that produces an eruption of wheals.
- ☐ 30. Herpes Zoster is a highly contagious viral infection that causes an eruptive, blister-like cluster.
- ☐ 31. Warts are most commonly found on feet, hands and fingers.

- ☐ 32. Rosacea is a chronic inflammatory condition of the face in which small capillaries of the face become dilated and inflamed.
- ☐ 33. Acne can be caused by genetics, emotional stress or hormonal changes.
- ☐ 34. Another name for a whitehead is a closed comedo.
- ☐ 35. Common myths about acne include: acne must just run its course, acne is caused by poor diet, and acne is caused by poor hygiene.
- ☐ 36. Benzoyl peroxide is an ingredient used to dry, exfoliate and help in killing bacteria.
- ☐ 37. Bromidrosis is a foul smelling perspiration caused by the yeast and bacteria that break down the sweat on the surface of the skin.
- ☐ 38. Skin tags are small elevated growths that can easily be removed by a physician.
- ☐ 39. Albinism is a congenital disease that results in the failure of the skin to produce melanin.
- ☐ 40. A nevus is a birthmark or congenital mole.
- ☐ 41. A freckle is called a lentigo.
- ☐ 42. Acute is the term used to identify intense and severe conditions and implies a rapid onset.
- ☐ 43. Chronic is the term used to describe symptoms that are frequent and continuing.
- ☐ 44. Edema is the swelling of tissue or skin caused by an excessive accumulation of fluid in the tissues.
- ☐ 45. Keratosis is the term for the buildup of skin cells on the epidermis.
- ☐ 46. Pruritus is an inflammation in the skin that causes severe itching, usually on undamaged skin.

- ☐ 47. A systemic disease is active internally throughout the body system.
- ☐ 48. Intrinsic aging is the natural aging process.
- ☐ 49. The amount of sun exposure the skin receives is the number one factor in extrinsic aging.
- ☐ 50. The general appearance of sun-damaged skin shows major structural changes including a leathery face, irregular pigment, a significant loss of elasticity and numerous fine lines and wrinkles.

Did You Know? CHAPTER 9 — Client Care
Check the box if you know the material.

☐ 1. Offering a friendly smile, making direct eye contact, extending your hand and shaking hands firmly and welcoming the client warmly and are ways to greet a client professionally and respectfully.

☐ 2. The telephone is usually the first contact a client has with the skin care center.

☐ 3. Eye contact is the nonverbal gesture that conveys undivided attention and demonstrates personal confidence.

☐ 4. Low key is the preferred tone of voice in professional settings.

☐ 5. The treatment record, personal skin evaluation and professional skin evaluation are components of the Client Consultation Form.

☐ 6. The personal information section of the Client Consultation Form asks for basic data that can be used to offer marketing promotions.

☐ 7. The medical history section of the Client Consultation Form identifies possible contraindication for particular products, equipment and services to be used or performed.

☐ 8. An allergen is a substance or ingredient likely to cause an allergic reaction.

☐ 9. Allergies to alpha and beta hydroxy acids can result in irritation.

☐ 10. Hyperpigmentation, acne and increased dryness are all possible side effects of hormone replacement therapy.

☐ 11. Epilepsy, pregnancy and pacemakers are all conditions that should avoid electrical current.

☐ 12. Dilated capillaries that can be treated with gentle massage and soothing, mild products is referred to as telangiectasia.

- ☐ 13. Any type of treatments should be avoided on clients with active Herpes Simplex lesions.
- ☐ 14. Dieting, exercising and smoking are all lifestyle factors that may affect the skin.
- ☐ 15. Smoking is a lifestyle factor that robs nutrients and oxygen from the skin.
- ☐ 16. Regular exercise promotes a healthy body and skin by increasing circulation.
- ☐ 17. The Client Release Statement may protect the skin care center for claims related to damage that may occur to the client's skin as a result of the services provided.
- ☐ 18. The professional skin evaluation is the part of the Client Consultation Form in which the esthetician reviews and evaluates the skin.
- ☐ 19. A professional skin analysis should be performed each visit.
- ☐ 20. Decreased wrinkles, improved hydration and improved pigmentation are indicators of an effective skin care treatment.
- ☐ 21. The size of the pores is most visible on the cheek area.
- ☐ 22. The key ingredient a product contains that makes it effective is referred to as the feature.
- ☐ 23. Asking the client to schedule another appointment in advance is referred to as rebooking.
- ☐ 24. Providing clients with a home care treatment plan, reviewing with clients the products used during the treatment and stressing the features and benefits of recommended products, are all steps that should be followed upon completion of the treatment.
- ☐ 25. A product statement is an explanation of what a product will do and why.
- ☐ 26. The results that the ingredients deliver are called benefits.

- ☐ 27. Retail accounts for 15% to 30% of service dollars.
- ☐ 28. You should strive to acquire 15% to 20% more new clients each week.
- ☐ 29. Word-of-mouth is the best form of advertising in any customer service business.
- ☐ 30. The recommended timeline for follow-up calls and notes is within 72 hours.

Did You Know? CHAPTER 10 — Facials
Check the box if you know the material.

☐ 1. Regular exercise, a well-balanced diet and an adequate intake of water are all elements of proper skin care that combine to result in healthy, glowing skin.

☐ 2. The basic regimen of cleansing, toning, moisturizing and protecting is recommended to be followed twice daily.

☐ 3. Cleansing is the first step in the basic skin care regimen specifically designed to remove dirt, oil, makeup and environmental pollutants from the surface of the skin.

☐ 4. Protecting is the final step of the basic skin care regimen that deals with the harmful UVA and UVB rays projected from the sun.

☐ 5. An SPF of 30 is recommended for sports or swimming when perspiration or water can wash away the sunscreen.

☐ 6. The most effective sunscreens contain ingredients that act as both blockers and absorbers.

☐ 7. A chemical exfoliant works in conjunction with other ingredients to cause a chemical reaction to remove dead skin cells.

☐ 8. Crème masks are ideal for dry skin types.

☐ 9. A modeling mask seals the skin, locking in moisture and creating a firm, taut feeling after removal.

☐ 10. Paraffin masks increase circulation and promote penetration of any nutrients or ingredients applied underneath it.

☐ 11. Massage is a systematic, therapeutic method of manipulating the body by rubbing, pinching, tapping, kneading and stroking.

☐ 12. Benefits of massage include tighter, firmer muscles, stronger muscle tissue and stimulation of glandular activities of the skin.

- ☐ 13. Effleurage is a light, relaxing, smooth, gentle, stroking or circular massage movement.
- ☐ 14. Petrissage is probably the most important of the massage movements.
- ☐ 15. Petrissage movements are used on the arms, shoulders and upper back.
- ☐ 16. Tapotement is the massage movement that is the most stimulating and is used for the shortest period of time.
- ☐ 17. Hacking is a massage motion that resembles a chopping movement using the edge of the hands.
- ☐ 18. Chucking is a form of friction performed by holding the client's arm in one hand and lifting the skin firmly up and down over the bone with the other hand.
- ☐ 19. Vibration is the shaking movement achieved when the esthetician quickly shakes his or her arms while the fingertips or palms are touching the client.
- ☐ 20. Contraindications for massage include heart conditions, previous stroke and high blood pressure.
- ☐ 21. Important points to remember about massage manipulations include checking for contraindications first, providing an even tempo or rhythm and pressure and practicing techniques on a mannequin head or on your knee.
- ☐ 22. A normal skin type displays few breakouts or clogged pores.
- ☐ 23. A dry skin type lacks sebum production and appears thin and delicate.
- ☐ 24. Oily skin types are less likely to display fine lines and wrinkles.
- ☐ 25. The most common skin type is combination.

- ☐ 26. Qualities of mature/aging skin include lack of firmness, increased dryness and apparent fine lines and wrinkles.
- ☐ 27. Couperose is a skin condition that displays fine dilated capillaries.
- ☐ 28. Rosacea is a vascular disorder characterized by flushed redness, dilated capillaries and small red bumps.
- ☐ 29. Acne is a skin condition caused by overactivity of sebaceous glands that generally occurs during adolescence.
- ☐ 30. If the esthetician suspects a medical condition, he or she should refer the client to a dermatologist or specialist.
- ☐ 31. An astringent assists in cleansing the skin and returns normal to dry skin to a normal pH.
- ☐ 32. A magnifying lamp provides a thorough examination of the skin's surface.
- ☐ 33. An infrared lamp relaxes the client and softens the skin to allow for penetration of a product.
- ☐ 34. A rotating brush allows for superficial exfoliation and deep cleansing of the skin.
- ☐ 35. Proper infection control procedures include keeping lids tightly closed on product jars, discarding any implements that cannot be disinfected and washing and sanitizing hands before and after every client.
- ☐ 36. Washing and sanitizing hands is the first step in performing a basic facial.
- ☐ 37. Desincrustation solution is a highly alkaline solution that liquefies sebum.
- ☐ 38. A mask should be left to set on the face for approximately 5 to 10 minutes.

☐ 39. After completing a basic facial, the esthetician should offer to book the client's next visit, recommend retail products to the client and arrange products and implements for the next service.

☐ 40. Indirect High Frequency current is used during massage to amplify the effects of the massage movements for relaxation and stimulation.

Did You Know? CHAPTER 11 — Hair Removal
Check the box if you know the material.

- ☐ 1. Shaving, tweezing and chemical depilatories are temporary hair removal procedures.
- ☐ 2. Hirsutism is caused by hormonal imbalances and typically affects women by causing dark hair to grow in areas of the body such as the face, arms, legs and back.
- ☐ 3. Excessive hair growth which is genetically determined is called hypertrichosis.
- ☐ 4. Capilli is hair that grows on the scalp.
- ☐ 5. Thick, coarse hair that grows on the face to form a beard is called barba.
- ☐ 6. Cilia is eyelash hair.
- ☐ 7. Supercilia is eyebrow hair.
- ☐ 8. Soft, downy hair on the body at birth is lanugo.
- ☐ 9. Vellus is thin, soft unpigmented hair that covers the body.
- ☐ 10. Thicker pigmented hair that grows on areas of the body after puberty is called terminal.
- ☐ 11. Anagen, catagen and telogen are all phases of the hair life cycle.
- ☐ 12. The anagen phase is the first and longest phase when the hair actively grows.
- ☐ 13. The stage in which the hair begins to destroy itself as it disconnects from the papilla is the catagen phase.
- ☐ 14. Telogen is the phase in which the hair sheds, and the follicle rests and prepares to resume to the anagen phase.
- ☐ 15. Shaving is a temporary hair removal technique. Hair usually grows back in 24 to 48 hours.
- ☐ 16. A patch test should be performed prior to application of a chemical depilatory. The main ingredient is derivative of thioglycolic acid, and regrowth of hair will occur within several days.

☐ 17. Chemical depilatories are generally left on the skin no more than 10 minutes.

☐ 18. Bleach chemically lightens hair by removing pigment.

☐ 19. Tweezing removes unwanted hair from smaller areas and is very beneficial in finishing the eyebrow design.

☐ 20. The most popular waxing service in the skin care center is the upper lip.

☐ 21. The majority of professional waxing services are performed with soft wax.

☐ 22. Hard wax is ideal for small areas and thinner more sensitive skin.

☐ 23. An ancient method of hair removal using a cotton thread is called threading.

☐ 24. Sugaring is a hair removal technique that involves applying a paste to the skin in a rolling motion.

☐ 25. The sugaring method of hair removal generally lasts 4 to 6 weeks.

☐ 26. Electrolysis is a method of hair removal that requires the technician to insert a small needle into each hair follicle.

☐ 27. A person who specializes in electrolysis is called an electrologist.

☐ 28. Proper training is necessity for preventing irreparable damage while performing any type of electrolysis.

☐ 29. Galvanic, thermolysis and blend are all methods of electrolysis.

☐ 30. The Galvanic method destroys the hair by using 12 to 14 needles to decompose the papilla.

☐ 31. Galvanic electrolysis is known as the "multiple needle" process.

☐ 32. Galvanic electrolysis destroys the hair by decomposing the papilla. Twelve to 14 needles are inserted into individual follicles at a time and a low-level current is on for 30 seconds to 2.5 minutes.

☐ 33. The thermolysis method involves inserting a single needle into the hair follicles.

☐ 34. During thermolysis a single needle is inserted into the follicles, the client feels a tiny "flash" of heat and current travels to the papilla.

☐ 35. The blend method consists of a combination of Galvanic and short-wave current.

☐ 36. The blend method offers the best results to clients with excessive or resistant hair growth.

☐ 37. Laser hair removal uses wavelengths of light to penetrate and diminish or destroy hair bulbs.

☐ 38. Laser treatment works best on hair that is in the anagen stage.

☐ 39. Photo-epilation hair removal uses a burst of energy that destroys hair bulbs, does not use a constant beam of light and can treat large areas of the body rapidly.

☐ 40. Wax remover eliminates wax residue from the skin.

☐ 41. A hair growth retardant slows the growth of hair after waxing.

☐ 42. Guidelines for safety and sanitation during waxing procedures include discarding anything that cannot be sanitized, performing a patch test prior to performing a service and testing the temperature of heated wax on your forearm before application.

☐ 43. Contraindications for waxing include sunburn, active Herpes and varicose veins.

☐ 44. Lupus is an autoimmune disease in which the body's immune system is impaired or begins to fight itself.

☐ 45. Washing and sanitizing your hands should be the first step taken in a basic waxing procedure.

Did You Know? CHAPTER 12 — Makeup

Check the box if you know the material.

- ☐ 1. The law of color states that, out of all the colors in the universe, only three are pure.
- ☐ 2. Yellow, red and blue are the primary colors.
- ☐ 3. The secondary color violet contains equal amounts of red and blue.
- ☐ 4. Mixing a primary color with a neighboring secondary color in equal proportions will produce a tertiary color.
- ☐ 5. Colors such as brown or gray are created by mixing primary, secondary and tertiary colors in unequal and equal proportions.
- ☐ 6. The position of a color on the color wheel demonstrates its relationship to the primary colors.
- ☐ 7. The complementary color scheme is used most often to enhance eye color.
- ☐ 8. Value is the lightness or darkness of a color.
- ☐ 9. The tone of a color is described as warm or cool.
- ☐ 10. Warm colors describe the tones of colors, contain red or yellow undertones and belong in the orange and red half of the color wheel.
- ☐ 11. The monochromatic color scheme uses the same color with variations in value and intensity throughout the entire makeup design.
- ☐ 12. Triadic color schemes are often used for more vibrant effects, are more dramatic than monochromatic or analog color schemes and use three colors located in a triangular position on the color wheel.
- ☐ 13. The ideal or classic facial shape is oval.
- ☐ 14. Contouring can appear to reshape the face, add the illusion of increased dimension to the face, and diminish the appearance of features with the use of dark colors.
- ☐ 15. Chiaroscuro is the art of arranging light and dark so as to produce the illusion of three-dimensional shapes.

☐ 16. A hint of contour should be added directly below the cheekbone in order to add dimension to an oblong face.

☐ 17. The pear-shaped face has a narrow forehead and a wide jawline.

☐ 18. Thin, sculpted arches create a dramatic effect in an eyebrow design.

☐ 19. Deep-set eyes require very little contouring because they are recessed.

☐ 20. Blending shadows in horizontal fashion, contouring and shading the protruding area and "grading" the shadow from dark at the lids to light as you approach the browbone are all makeup applications that benefit bulging eyes.

☐ 21. A fuller appearance for thin lips can be created by using lip liner to draw a line beyond the natural fullness of the lip.

☐ 22. The ideal lighting for makeup application is fluorescent and incandescent.

☐ 23. The facial chair should not recline more than 45° when applying makeup.

☐ 24. The use of foundation can correct undesirable skin tones, conceal imperfections on the skin, and help protect skin from UV-related damage.

☐ 25. Liquid foundation is the most common form of foundation and is generally preferred because of its sheer, natural coverage and easy application and blending.

☐ 26. Skin type, time of year and type of finish required are all important factors to consider when selecting a foundation.

☐ 27. Unless correction is required, the general guideline is to match foundation to the skin tone.

☐ 28. A golden skin tone has a yellow cast.

☐ 29. Light peach foundation should be used for a blue/violet undertone.

- ☐ 30. Concealer can correct under-eye circles, broken capillaries, blemishes and dark, shadowed areas of the face.
- ☐ 31. "Wide-set" eyes have a space between the eyes greater than the width of one eye.
- ☐ 32. The area between the base of the lashes and the crease line makes up 1/3 of the eye.
- ☐ 33. Liquid and powder eyeliners are usually applied with a brush.
- ☐ 34. Mascara defines, thickens and lengthens the eyelashes.
- ☐ 35. The lip color should not overpower the amount of color applied to the cheeks and eyes.
- ☐ 36. Lipstick is the most common type of lip color.
- ☐ 37. Toner purifies and balances the skin's pH levels.
- ☐ 38. Exfoliator is a product that removes excess surface skin cells.
- ☐ 39. Eyeliner is a makeup product that accentuates and defines the shape of the eyes.
- ☐ 40. The purpose of lip liner is to define or correct the shape of the lips.
- ☐ 41. A spatula is used to remove the product from the container.
- ☐ 42. Tweezers are used for shaping eyebrows, removing stray hairs and applying artificial lashes.
- ☐ 43. A makeup application is 80% art and 20% science.
- ☐ 44. A victim of a fire, a cancer survivor and a client with congenital disfigurement would all be prospective clients for a camouflage makeup.
- ☐ 45. It takes approximately 30 minutes to perform an eyelash and eyebrow tinting procedure.

Did You Know? CHAPTER 13 — Advanced Treatments
Check the box if you know the material.

☐ 1. Contraindications for performing a treatment include sunburn, fungal infections and high blood pressure.

☐ 2. A mask is used to hydrate, calm and soothe the skin.

☐ 3. An exfoliant softens skin by removing dead skin cells.

☐ 4. Gomage is an exfoliating treatment in which a layer of crème is applied to the skin, allowed to dry and then rubbed away.

☐ 5. The principles of absorption and compaction give wraps the ability to create temporary tightness.

☐ 6. Prior to a body wrap, bandages may be soaked in an aromatherapy toning solution.

☐ 7. Cellophane is used to wrap the body and increase product penetration and treatment results.

☐ 8. Affusion therapy is a method of water therapy in which the client is sprayed with water, seawater or mineral water infused with herbs or essential oils.

☐ 9. Superficial or light chemical peels affect only the epidermis.

☐ 10. Microdermabrasion is a treatment that offers a light resurfacing of the epidermis.

☐ 11. The degree of exfoliation during microdermabrasion depends on the level of crystal spray, the number of passes over the skin and the number of treatments performed.

☐ 12. Approximately 6 to 12 microdermabrasion treatments are required to achieve noticeable improvement.

☐ 13. Dermabrasion is a treatment that requires a patient to be anesthetized.

☐ 14. If the client's skin is noticeably pink after the first pass of the microdermabrasion machine over the face, the esthetician should not perform a second pass.

☐ 15. The esthetician should advise the client to avoid saunas and steam for 24 to 48 hours following a microdermabrasion treatment.

☐ 16. Reflexology is a technique that uses finger-point pressure to influence certain body conditions.

☐ 17. Lymph is a fluid responsible for delivering nutrients to cells and carrying away cellular waste before it becomes toxic to the body.

☐ 18. Manual lymphatic drainage massage (MLD) treatment uses a gentle pumping technique to help eliminate toxins, waste and excess water from the face and body.

☐ 19. Cellulite massage treatments increase circulation, promote the removal of excess fluids and waste material and firm the muscle tissue.

☐ 20. Phytotherapy refers to the medicinal use of plants.

☐ 21. Active ingredients are chemicals such as alkaloids and glucosides that give plants their healing properties.

☐ 22. An analgesic relieves pain either by relaxing muscles or reducing pain signals to the brain.

☐ 23. An antimicrobial is a natural substance that is responsible for killing a wide range of harmful bacteria, fungi and viruses.

☐ 24. An antiseptic is a natural substance that prevents bacterial growth on the skin with external application.

☐ 25. An astringent provides a constricting, drying effect and helps contract tissue and reduce secretions.

☐ 26. Circulatory stimulants are natural substances that increase blood flow at the surface of the skin.

- ☐ 27. An emollient is a natural substance that softens, soothes and protects skin.
- ☐ 28. Tinctures are commercial extractions that require soaking an herb in alcohol to extract the active ingredient from the plant.
- ☐ 29. An ointment is a thick crème or salve made from the combination of herbs and petroleum.
- ☐ 30. An infusion is created by steeping an herb in boiling water.
- ☐ 31. Soaking a clean towel in the liquid from both an infusion and decoction and applying it to a specific area of the body is known as fomentation.
- ☐ 32. Aromatherapy is the controlled use of essential oils.
- ☐ 33. The floral category of fragrance is the easiest to identify.
- ☐ 34. Floral bouquet is the largest category of fragrance.
- ☐ 35. Examples of scents in the fruit blend category of fragrance include apple, melon and pomegranate.
- ☐ 36. The modern blend category of fragrance represents concoctions from several different scents.
- ☐ 37. Antiseptic oils help destroy bacteria and heal skin eruptions.
- ☐ 38. Anti-inflammatory oils reduce inflammation and soothe swollen muscles.
- ☐ 39. Healing oils promote cells to regenerate so the skin can repair itself.
- ☐ 40. Moisturizing oils are responsible for softening dry or flaky skin.
- ☐ 41. Steam distillation is the most common method for obtaining essential oils.
- ☐ 42. Expression is a common method for obtaining essential oils that involves squeezing out an ingredient's fragrant oil.

☐ 43. Commercial extraction is a method for obtaining essential oils that uses a chemical solvent to leach the aromatic component from an ingredient.

☐ 44. Tea tree is an essential oil that is often used in treating acne.

☐ 45. Sandalwood is an essential oil used in therapies aimed at treating sore muscles.

Did You Know? CHAPTER 14 — Estheticians in the Medical Field
Check the box if you know the material.

☐ 1. A dermatologist is a physician who specializes in diagnosing and treating diseases of the skin and nails.

☐ 2. Peeling, shedding and coming off in scales are all properties of desquamation of the stratum corneum.

☐ 3. A light peel can be performed by an esthetician in a skin care center.

☐ 4. The EMDA is the agency that has established procedural guidelines to ensure safety and consistency in the use of alpha hydroxy acids (AHAs) for chemical peels.

☐ 5. Regardless of the type of peel performed, direct sun exposure must be avoided for one month following the treatment.

☐ 6. Chemical peels are recommended for fair skin with superficial wrinkles.

☐ 7. Deep peels are recommended for treating deep facial wrinkles, sun-damaged skin and uneven pigmentation.

☐ 8. Collagen or fat injection treatments fill in creased, furrowed or sunken facial skin, lines and wrinkles.

☐ 9. Collagen or fat injections usually last for 3-6 months.

☐ 10. Collagen or fat injections add fullness to lips, plump up facial skin and decrease indentations of the skin.

☐ 11. Fat injections are used to treat sunken cheeks, laugh lines, skin depressions or indentations, forehead wrinkles or to enlarge lips.

☐ 12. Dermabrasion procedures improve uneven skin textures by mechanically scraping off the top layers of the skin.

☐ 13. Dermabrasion is used to treat acne scars, pigmentation and deep wrinkles.

☐ 14. Blepharoplasty or eyelid surgery is used to remove excess fat, skin or muscle from the upper and lower eyelids.

☐ 15. Tightness of the eyelids, excessive tearing and temporary blurred vision are all side-effects of blepharoplasty.

☐ 16. Blepharoplasty is recommended for patients with drooping upper eyelids or puffy bags below the eyes.

☐ 17. Rhytidectomy can improve visible signs of aging by removing excess fat, tightening underlying muscles and re-draping the skin of the face and neck.

☐ 18. Rhytidectomy is recommended for individuals whose face and neck have begun to sag but still have some elasticity in their facial skin and good bone structure.

☐ 19. Reduction of jowls, making loose neck skin more taut and improvement of sagging facial skin are all results of rhytidectomy.

☐ 20. Laser resurfacing uses a beam of highly focused light to vaporize the upper layers of damaged skin at specific and controlled levels of penetration.

☐ 21. Ablative lasers remove the affected portion of the epidermis to heat the papillary dermis, to regenerate collagen.

☐ 22. Laser resurfacing is recommended for patients seeking treatment for fine lines.

☐ 23. A laser resurfacing patient should wait 2 weeks before returning to normal activities.

☐ 24. A bacterial infection is a post-operative complication that can develop when microbes invade an inured, open or wounded part of the body.

☐ 25. A yeast infection is a superficial infection that occurs on moist areas of the skin.

☐ 26. Herpetic infection is a highly contagious viral infection that is triggered when the body or skin is placed under extreme stress, such as a laser treatment.

☐ 27. Conjunctivitis is a post-operative complication that has undesirable side-effects such as having red, itchy and watery eyes that may develop a significant amount of pus.

☐ 28. Yeast infection is a post-operative complication that includes extreme redness and clusters or large patches of pustules which can later develop into scaly patches.

☐ 29. Ecchymosis is the clinical term for bruising.

☐ 30. Erythema is the clinical term for redness.

☐ 31. First-degree burns are the least severe and they only damage the epidermis.

☐ 32. Second-degree burns penetrate to the dermis, resulting in redness, swelling and blistering.

☐ 33. To care for a second-degree burn, the burned area should be immersed in cool water.

☐ 34. The most severe burn which damages or destroys underlying tissue, exposes nerve endings, and burns fat, muscle and bone is a third-degree burn.

☐ 35. Skin grafting is taking a section of healthy skin from an unburned area of the body and surgically reattaching it to cover the burned area.

☐ 36. Third-degree burns are frequently treated with an antimicrobial dressing.

☐ 37. Keratolytic medications, antibacterial medications and anti-inflammatory medications are all examples of topical medications.

☐ 38. Anti-inflammatory medications are used to treat inflammatory conditions such as dermatitis.

☐ 39. Crèmes or ointments used to promote rapid cell turnover and exfoliation are referred to as keratolytic medications.

☐ 40. Antibacterial types of medications are used to kill bacteria and prevent them from reproducing.

☐ 41. Systemic medications are taken orally and travel through the body in the bloodstream.

☐ 42. Antibiotics are a type of systemic medication that is used to kill or prevent the growth of bacteria.

☐ 43. An antihistamine is frequently prescribed to relieve uncomfortable skin conditions such as itching and hives.

☐ 44. A TCA-chemical peel would most likely require additional training and/or working under a physician's supervision.

☐ 45. The procedures that may be legally performed, as defined by a local regulatory agency is referred to as the scope of practice.